24K LIFE

24K LIFE

Living Every Day Refined By God's Word

LeeAnn Kirkindoll

ELM HILL

A Division of
HarperCollins Christian Publishing

www.elmhillbooks.com

24k Life
Living Every Day Refined By God's Word

Published in Nashville, Tennessee, by Elm Hill, an imprint of Thomas Nelson. Elm Hill and Thomas Nelson are registered trademarks of HarperCollins Christian Publishing, Inc.

Elm Hill titles may be purchased in bulk for educational, business, fund-raising, or sales promotional use. For information, please e-mail SpecialMarkets@ThomasNelson.com.

Scripture quotations marked ESV are from the ESV® Bible (The Holy Bible, English Standard Version®). Copyright © 2001 by Crossway, a publishing ministry of Good News Publishers. Used by permission. All rights reserved.

Scripture quotations marked GNT are from the Good News Translation in Today's English Version—Second Edition. Copyright 1992 by American Bible Society. Used by permission.

Scripture quotations marked HCSB are from the Holman Christian Standard Bible®. Copyright © 1999, 2000, 2002, 2003, 2009 by Holman Bible Publishers. Used by permission. HCSB® is a federally registered trademark of Holman Bible Publishers.

Scripture quotations marked KJV are from the King James Version. Public domain.

Scripture quotations marked NASB are from New American Standard Bible®. Copyright © 1960, 1962, 1963, 1968, 1971, 1972, 1973, 1975, 1977, 1995 by The Lockman Foundation. Used by permission. (www.Lockman.org)

Scripture quotations marked NIV are from the Holy Bible, New International Version®, NIV®. Copyright © 1973, 1978, 1984, 2011 by Biblica, Inc.® Used by permission of Zondervan. All rights reserved worldwide. www.Zondervan.com. The "NIV" and "New International Version" are trademarks registered in the United States Patent and Trademark Office by Biblica, Inc.®

Scripture quotations marked NKJV are from the New King James Version®. © 1982 by Thomas Nelson. Used by permission. All rights reserved.

Scripture quotations marked NLT are from the Holy Bible, New Living Translation. © 1996, 2004, 2007, 2013, 2015 by Tyndale House Foundation. Used by permission of Tyndale House Publishers, Inc., Carol Stream, Illinois 60188. All rights reserved.

Scripture quotations marked THE MESSAGE are from *The Message*. Copyright © by Eugene H. Peterson 1993, 1994, 1995, 1996, 2000, 2001, 2002. Used by permission of NavPress. All rights reserved. Represented by Tyndale House Publishers, Inc.

Scripture quotations marked TLB are from The Living Bible. Copyright © 1971. Used by permission of Tyndale House Publishers, Inc., Carol Stream, Illinois 60188. All rights reserved.

Library of Congress Cataloging-in-Publication Data

Library of Congress Control Number: 2019919047

ISBN 978-1-400325870 (Paperback)
ISBN 978-1-400325887 (Hardbound)
ISBN 978-1-400325894 (eBook)

Special Thanks

I would like to give a special thanks to my friend and editor, Kevin Stewart, for the hours upon hours he dedicated to this project—whether by phone, computer, or his famous "yellow highlighter". Kevin, you have been more than just a partner that corrects my grammar and sentence structure. Your faith in my vision and your words of encouragement, throughout this project, have played an integral part in successfully putting the lessons I've learned on paper. My prayer is that our hard work will go on to help others refine their hearts—just as God has surely refined ours using the words on these pages. Gary and I love you more than I can express—and that is saying a lot coming from a gal who's nickname is 'Gabby'. Here's to you, friend! You truly are SOLID GOLD in 'my book'. (Wink, Wink!)

Love Always,
LeeAnn

Special Dedication

This book is dedicated with great love to my precious husband, Gary. Thank you for all of your love and support throughout this project. I am blessed to be your wife. To my precious children and grands, I pray that you will be blessed by these words and be affirmed of God's love and pursuit of you, personally. Always know how dearly loved you are by me. You are my pride and joy and no one on this earth could love you more.

TABLE OF CONTENTS

Digging Deeper

We pray that the book you're holding in your hands will be a blessing in your life. However, you have a chance to study at a deeper level as well! Our ultimate goal is that the photos, devotions and the specific opportunities for life application found in the FREE **24k Gold Digger's Study Guide** will all work together to plant a lasting memory of the nuggets found in **24k Life**. When all three are combined, these refinements in your daily relationship with Jesus Christ will have enduring effects. It might be that God brings a photo to your memory when you need to be reminded of a promise. A scripture memorized could prompt a move toward faith instead of fear when your heart is troubled. When action is taken in regards to the concepts you study, life-changing results will be evident in your life that positively affect others too. So take a moment and see how you can dig a little deeper with us!

Before you get started:

*Go to LeeAnnKirkindoll.com and download the FREE **24k Life Gold Digger's Study Guide**

*The **24k Life Gold Digger's Study Guide** provides opportunities to dig deeper into God's Word as well as practical ways to apply what you are currently reading in the book. Each is a different and unique 'lesson' to enhance your study of the information in **24k Life**. Every week holds something different than the week before. You won't get bored!

*The **24k Life Devotional** can be used as a *daily* Devotional or a *weekly* Bible Study.

*You can study on your own or with a group.

*Follow LeeAnnKirkindoll on Instagram and Facebook to stay informed about more **24k Life** goodies and extras.

How to use this book as a Study:

1) Read the **24k Life Devotion** entry.
2) Highlight the scripture for that entry in your Bible.
3) Spend time that day/week memorizing one of the scriptures in the Study Guide that correlates with the devotion entry you are studying.
4) Follow the guidelines for deeper study in your downloaded **24k Life Gold Digger's Study Guide** for that particular devotional.
5) Follow through PERSONALLY on any practical life application prompts in the Devotional and Study Guide.
6) Be sure to share what you are learning on your social media platforms and bring others along with you in this quest to be refined by Christ.

Note from LeeAnn

Hey There! Chances are, you probably don't know me yet...but I'm hoping that our hearts will be connected by the time we've completed this devotional together. And, because I'm counting on you and me getting to know one another better over virtual cups of coffee as God refines us, I will go ahead and let you in on a well-known fact about me that everyone *who does know me already* understands: I have a love affair going on with shiny things. Yep, I'm a sucker for anything that sparkles and shines—in fact, you should see the grin on my face as I'm typing this. And when it comes to gold, well let's just say, it's at the top of my list of shiny favorites! So, it's really no surprise that God would provide an opportunity for me to write a devotional full of lessons inspired by photos of things that are GOLD.

At the beginning of every new year, I ask the Lord to give me a 'word' that will stand out in my life over the next twelve months. One that will challenge me to learn more. One that will "show up" in my daily interactions as I grow in my faith. A word that will transform my life in unexpected ways, leaving me a little wiser in December than I was in January. This particular year, God gave me the word PERSPECTIVE. And as you can imagine, it has not disappointed! But little did I realize—when I began to focus in on this eleven letter word—it would end up being the driving force behind the book you are about to read.

24k Life is filled with stories, lessons and hope—all direct results of allowing God to refine my heart and my motives so that I can better see things from His perspective. Each entry is a challenge to let the messiness of our daily lives intersect with the refining truth of God's Word. Every devotion was inspired by a photo that immediately brought a particular spiritual lesson to the forefront of my mind. Some are quick nudges toward actions required to show the love of Christ in our day to day routines. Others are more lengthy as we seek to change mindsets that have kept us paralyzed in fear or stuck in old habits that rob our opportunities to reflect Christ. Each entry stands on its own and is meant to be focused on throughout your week with scripture memory, deeper personal study and life application. You will find that I write the same way I talk—and I do that on purpose. As you read, I want you to feel like we are two friends having a conversation and sharing our stories. Want to know why that is important to me?

Just like you, I struggle with handling disappointment. To trust God with the "un-trustables". To see things from His perspective. But I also hope that you, *just like me,* are ready to let God refine those areas that need a little work. That you have a heart that wants to see Him use your life to draw others to His unfailing love. If you have never met Jesus personally, I pray you find Him in the pages of these stories and entries because He loves you so much. It's life-changing to learn that when our mindsets meet God's point of view, the opportunity to emerge as 24k—solid gold, without blemish, luminous and refined to its purest state—actually becomes a reality. No matter your circumstances. No matter where you currently are. No matter where you used to be. Today can be the day to emerge as GOLD.

> *"But He knows where I'm going. And when He tests me, I will come out as PURE GOLD...I have obeyed every word He's spoken, and not just obeyed His advice—I've treasured it."*
>
> *JOB 23:10,11B NLT, THE MESSAGE*

So how about it? Are you ready to become a modern day "Gold Digger"? There are nuggets and treasures galore found within the pages of our Bibles. This GOLD will not only enrich our lives but also the lives of others. I don't know about you, but that sounds like a win-win to me! So grab a shovel—and a journal.

Oh! And don't forget a cozy beverage of your choice!

Then let's lock 'hearts' and live this 24k Life—together.

Keep It Shiny Gals,

"I will bring that group through the fire and make them pure. I will refine them like silver and purify them like gold. They will call on my name, and I will answer them. I will say, "These are my people," and they will say, "The LORD is our God.""

ZECHARIAH 13:9

FOOL'S GOLD

DAY 1

"But test everything; hold fast to what is good."

1 THESSALONIANS 5:21 ESV

L et's begin today with a short geology lesson that just may hold a little more meaning for us today than it did in our sixth grade science class.

The mineral, Pyrite, is an iron sulfide with the chemical formula FeS_2. It is considered the most common of the sulfide minerals. It's metallic luster and pale brass-yellow hue give it a superficial resemblance to gold, giving this mineral it's well-known nickname of "fool's gold". Pyrite may be shiny and gold-colored, but any miner will tell you, it cannot compare to the value of *real gold*. The fact is that real gold can be worth over $1,700 per ounce, while you'll be lucky to get a dollar for that much Pyrite. The most frustrating part? This gold 'knock-off' has a chance to fool so many because it's more commonly found and it's often discovered near sources of real gold.

In light of this information, there is a question that begs to be asked. When someone comes across us in life, are they finding a "precious" metal—meaning THE REAL THING—or a knock-off that will end up disappointing them in the end? Interestingly enough, we can follow the same tests a miner would use to examine whether or not she's found real gold or fool's gold. Here are a few qualities that help differentiate this valuable treasure from its less valued but more prevalent knock-off.

RARITY: Fool's gold can be found in abundance. It takes digging though the "imposters" to find the actual gold.

SHINE: When you're viewing fool's gold with the natural eye, it will glisten, not shine. Gold shines at any angle, not just when the "light is right".

HARDNESS: Fool's gold is much harder and more brittle than gold. Gold is softer and more pliable in makeup where fool's gold leaves scratches behind.

COLOR: Fool's gold is naturally not as brilliant in color as real gold. When it is crushed, it actually turns a blackish-green color instead of keeping its metallic appearance. When gold is crushed into powder, its brilliant gold luster stays the same.

RESIDUE: When tested, gold will leave a pure yellow trail of residue behind while fool's gold will leave a black powdery substance.

EDGES: Fool's gold is characterized by its sharp edges. Gold has more rounded surfaces and is recognized as being softer to the touch.

What about you? If you were held to a gold standard, how would you "pan out"? Are you a 'dime-a-dozen' imposter posing as the real thing? Are you only "shiny" from certain angles? When you rub up against others in life, is an encounter with you abrasive or soft? When things are "crushing" you in life, do you 'change colors' or stay a brilliant reflection of the gold you carry? When you've spent time with others, what are you leaving behind? Is it a trail of solid gold they could follow or a dark imprint that reminds them that they didn't encounter what they set out to find?

On this journey to be refined by God, these are great ways to measure our progress. Just remember this. If you are hoping to be found as gold by others, it must begin by digging and finding this treasure for yourself. And I think it's only fair to warn you. The hunt for "gold' within scripture is going to call for some tenacity. So, get ready. Oh! And beware. Chances are, throughout this expedition, you are going to get distracted by plenty of 'fool's gold' along the way. Just don't let it deter you from continuing your search for the real thing! Instead, embrace 'gold digging' as a way of life. Then you will be wise. Only the miner who stops digging once she has a piece of Pyrite in her hand becomes a 'fool'.

So, here's to all the "GOLD DIGGERS"! I pray that this devotional will be as a treasured tool in your personal refinement process. May each quest within the pages of God's Word be bountiful! May you be blessed beyond measure by the gold nuggets awaiting YOU in scripture for they have profound value and will add immeasurable worth to your life. And most importantly, be sure to share this treasure with the world—*by living out these truths*—so others can also be beneficiaries of the wealth you've found!

Heavenly Father, as I begin this journey to be refined by You, I give You permission to smooth out my rough edges and work on my shine. I want to be an authentic example of what a believer in Jesus Christ should look like—not an imposter or a cheap knock-off that is sure to disappoint. Do such a purifying work in me that my life produces 24k gold—something valued and treasured and worth searching for. Only You could bring forth something so precious—and then allow me the privilege of giving it away. I can't wait to be more like You. Amen

LET IT GO

"Cast all your anxieties on him, because he cares for you."

1 PETER 5:7 *NIV*

It's interesting. I've never considered myself to be a physically strong person. What about you? But not too long ago, body strength became the topic of conversation with a good friend. She said with confidence, "my legs are where I'm strongest." My response back to her was, "Well, actually, I'm not strong in any area!" We both started laughing because she knows all too well that I'm not a fitness fanatic. Later that day, I kept finding that conversation rolling around in my mind. The longer I thought about it, the more I realized that I could potentially be stronger than anyone I know in one specific area that I'd never considered before. Unfortunately, stronger than I ever desired to be—and that's MY GRIP.

I have a ridiculously strong grip. And I do believe, God isn't bragging about me to all of the angels in heaven about this supernatural strength, either. I don't know about you, but my grip is so tight on the things I hold dear. The people I love. The hopes I have. The future I desire. But rather than God saying, "Good girl! Way to go!" Instead He's saying, "Loosen that grip and... LET. IT. GO. Not like the infamous movie theme song where out of frustration, you just aren't going to care anymore. But just the opposite. When we "let it go" within the boundaries of God's loving request, we simultaneously let it all fall into the hands of a God who not only KNOWS MORE but even CARES MORE about those precious details we are trying to control.

What makes it so hard to just open up our clenched fists and give our "stuff" to God? It's worth addressing because our 'control' of everything is a myth anyway. God, himself, is the only one who holds control of it all. So, can we tackle letting go of some things together? Let's invite God to speak to our hearts and then practice the following: Let's loosen our grip. Let's let the cares of this world fall like glitter floating from the palms of our open hands. Do you realize that not one of those treasured 'sparkles' will hit the ground? Our God is there to catch every hope and every dream and place them in HIS sovereign grip.

Dear one, take heart. We can be assured of His love for us in this process. Because, though He asks us to let them go, we can take comfort in the fact that they fall directly into THE HANDS of THE ONE that will never let US go.

Father God, I ask that the enemy have no jurisdiction in my mind—convincing me to try and control every situation and outcome. I ask that if my grip is flexed, that it would be tightly attached to you instead of the people and things of this world. Let today be the day that I LET IT GO—whatever "it" is. And when I start to pick it back up, will You please remind me to lay it back down again? AND AGAIN, if I must? I'm thankful that the God I serve can be trusted with everything I hold dear. Amen

PROCLAMATIONS

DAY 3

"My thoughts are nothing like your thoughts," says the Lord.
"And my ways are far beyond anything you could imagine.
For just as the heavens are higher than the earth,
so my ways are higher than your ways and my
thoughts higher than your thoughts."

ISAIAH 55:8-9 NLT

Have you been waiting a long time for God to answer a prayer? Has it ever felt as if He may have forgotten you? I know I have experienced difficult seasons like that—and I think we can all agree on how exasperating that can be. My frustration over the unknown has led me down some very unfruitful paths. I've questioned God's love for me and I have questioned His sovereignty. I have even, unintentionally, found myself wanting to help God not 'lose face' in front of others by trying to explain to them why He hadn't answered my prayers the way it seemed He should. These explanations would include statements like: "I can see now that the reason He must have us 'in this place' is because ...." or "I believe He is trying to teach me something about...." or maybe even something like, "The enemy wants to take us down, but I know God is going to do 'this' in the end." Though some of these statements could

6

be true, they would be pure speculation. Thankfully, God loved me too much to leave me with a faulty mindset. I'm not going to lie. It stung a little at first. But it's changed my perspective on God's expectations for me as I wait for Him to answer my prayers. I hope it will help you 'adjust your expression of trust' on a more accurate level too.

Job answered God:
"I'm convinced: You can do anything and everything.
Nothing and no one can upset your plans.
You asked, 'Who is this muddying the water,
ignorantly confusing the issue, second-guessing my purposes?'
"I admit it. I was the one. I babbled on about things far beyond me,
made small talk about wonders way over my head."
You told me, 'Listen, and let me do the talking.
Let me ask the questions. You give the answers.'
I admit I once lived by rumors of you;
now I have it all firsthand—from my own eyes and ears!
I'm sorry—forgive me. I'll never do that again, I promise!
I'll never again live on crusts of hearsay, crumbs of rumor."
JOB 42:1-6 THE MESSAGE

It's important to remember here that Job had been through hell on earth at this point in their conversation. He had lost everything—possessions, health, position and his family. And to make matters worse, he had to endure the judgmental statements of his friends throughout this painful process. All of this with no good answer of "why" in sight. But just like Job, we need to continue to submit to God even when we don't know what He is doing in our moments of waiting. And we need to accept that it's okay to not have an 'acceptable answer' to give to those looking on either.

Personally, I had to address the fact that I was on a 'need to know basis' with God, but He was not on a 'need to share basis' with me. I'm now embracing the fact that the greatest peace comes from knowing that in many instances, we won't understand 'the why' until long after the process is over. Some may be insights we won't understand until we get to heaven! I'm learning that He wants us to spend more time listening to the truth of His Word than trying to figure Him out—that reverence of Him is more valuable than trying to bring His wisdom down to our level of understanding. In fact, that "peace that surpasses all understanding" (Phil 4:7, NKJV) is not found in the answers to my questions. Instead, it's found in the one who holds the answers. The more we look to the 'answer-giver' rather than the answer to our questions, the stronger our personal testimony of His character will be. God's desired result for us? We won't be living off the "crumbs" of what He has taught someone else.

When I began to practice my understanding of this truth, an interesting thing happened. My prior 'explanations' of God's involvement in my life instead turned into 'proclamations'. These professions of faith began to sound more like this: "I have no idea what is going on, but I know God is good. I know the plans He has for me. His Word says He will guide me, rescue me and give me strength to persevere. I'm allowing Him to deepen my trust in Him more and more every day in this situation." Those words point others to an all-powerful God—-unlike our wimpy 'explanations' of what we think He is doing—which only cause speculation for those within earshot.

So, examine yourself today. Are your responses to God's part in your "unanswered prayers" EXPLANATIONS OR PROCLAMATIONS? Are you guilty of "babbling on about things way over your head"? It truly matters. Others need the truth of God's intentions toward you—and ultimately them. And you know, once God and Job got things ironed out, God restored Job and blessed him with more than He originally had. He has YOUR BEST INTERESTS in mind as well. Spend more time talking about your faith than your fear. Proclaim His goodness. God is good all the time. All the time, God is good.

Jesus, you are a good, good Father. Disappointment and unanswered prayers do not change the character of an UNCHANGING GOD. Forgive me for trying to bring Your level of wisdom down to my limited understanding of the bigger picture. I want to proclaim your goodness each and every day—no matter what—so people will know the truth about who You are—not a warped version that makes me feel better about my uncomfortable circumstances. No one desires a gold-plated version of You. They need the 24k ALL POWERFUL ORIGINAL. Amen

WHAT'S YOUR GAME?

DAY 4

"Whoever conceals his transgressions will not prosper, but he who confesses and forsakes them will obtain mercy."

PROV 28:13 ESV

Excuses, excuses, excuses. We are all full of them, right? Or if we aren't full of them, we FOR SURE know someone who is. We've heard them all:

"It's not my fault!"

"I couldn't help it!"

"Everybody else is doing it!"

"Nobody's perfect!"

"I was pressured into it!"

But it isn't fair!"

or the most famous of all: "The devil made me do it!"

(Cue the eye roll followed by laying your forehead in your hand)

Our world today is engaged in a pretty mean round of the 'blame game' and it's definitely taking its toll on the 'players'. It's so easy to get in the habit of blaming others as well as making excuses for bad thoughts, poor decisions, procrastination and our own disobedience. For many of us, we are guilty of believing that everyone else is to blame for our harsh words, nasty attitudes and reckless social media account posts. But if we are going to be like GOLD, pliable, moldable and refined to our purest state, we are going to have to measure this destructive habit against the truth of God's Word—along with learning to recognize the enemy's rules of engagement.

My husband and I have been studying the difference between conviction and condemnation the past few weeks and the contrasts between them are worth noting. Conviction comes from the Lord and it's always specific to a particular action. Condemnation comes from the evil one and it's always vague with lots of room for assumptions, lack of reality and denial—which keeps us defeated. The enemy wants not only for you to be condemning of others, he also wants you to feel as though God looks forward to condemning you when you've missed the mark. However, that couldn't be further from the truth. He sent the Holy Spirit to be our guide. To whisper in our ear—or sometimes yell with a megaphone when it's more effective—when we need to see our actions for what they truly are. Only conviction from the Holy Spirit leads us to healthy changes in perspective. God wants to see us be powerful influencers, not obnoxious fault-finders that no one wants to 'play with'. So, ask the Lord to help you recognize the difference! A friend of mine made a statement worth quoting one night in our small group:

"Yes, the truth does hurt; but it will also set you free."

T. Traylor

There truly is freedom and room for great personal growth when we not only OWN OUR ACTIONS, but our REACTIONS too. Let God do all the necessary refining in your mindset that's needed. Give Him room to call "foul" when you start bending the rules. Be willing to make some changes in strategy when you realize you're playing a game you can't win. Let's all ditch the 'blame game' for some Uno or a rowdy game of Wahoo instead! No doubt—they're both a whole lot more fun to play.

Heavenly Father, it can be so hard to admit when I am wrong. It feels so much better at the time to push my guilt on someone else rather than admit my own. But I am also learning that I basically give the enemy a baseball bat to beat me with later whenever I choose that course of action, rather than deal with my shortcomings. Lord, you want me to be free of the bondage that results from always blaming others. So, help me to own my choices and offer apologies when needed. I want to be a blessing—not a bummer. Amen

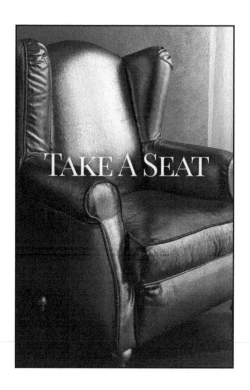

DAY 5

"Here's what I want you to do: Find a quiet, secluded place so you
won't be tempted to role-play before God. Just be there as simply
and honestly as you can manage. The focus will shift from you to
God, and you will begin to sense his grace."

MATTHEW 6:6 THE MESSAGE

One night, as I lay tucked in bed formulating my "to do list" for the following day, the picture of a gold chair kept coming to mind. And every time it did, I felt the Lord say, "Take a seat." With each task I added to my list, I'd hear it again. As my project list got longer, the reminder from the Lord became clearer: "No matter what needs to be accomplished tomorrow, remember that taking a seat with Me is the first priority." And I would add, it didn't feel like a suggestion. This reminder was anything but gentle and was uncompromisingly direct. It was definitely not: "Hey, I know how busy you are, and I realize there are only so many hours in a day. So, if you can fit me in, would you consider spending some time with me?" Nope. It was: "TAKE A SEAT." That simple and that direct.

So, this is the challenge: TAKE A SEAT and spend time with God EVERY DAY. Don't kid yourself into thinking you can maintain your fellowship with Him by reading a quick devo a day to keep the devil away! Don't be tricked into thinking that throwing up a desperate—maybe even last minute—prayer or listening to a great podcast in the middle of doing 20 other things will give you any sense of real peace. It's finding time at some point every day so you can sit still and be quiet before Him. For some, it may be on your closet floor while your kids are napping. For others, early in the morning. While for some it's in the evening once you finish with the events of the day and prepare to take on the next. But the goal is to spend focused quality time getting to know the Creator.

Relationships on earth must be developed to be meaningful. Our relationships with Jesus are no different. So, develop that relationship. Choose it over TV. Choose it instead of a good novel. Prioritize it above a phone call. Let it replace your time on social media. Allow 'the sometimes awkward silence' of just being still and quiet—alone in His presence with your Bible open—to shift your focus from "your world" to God. From "your fear" to God. From "your disappointment" to God. From "your loneliness" to God. From "your doubt" to God. From "your exhaustion" to God. That time with Him will be golden. Friend, you've been given the best seat in the house. Make sure you take advantage of it!

Lord, I confess that my busy schedule works overtime to steal my time with you. But I also know how much my heart needs to be mended and my soul strengthened. May I be found sitting at your feet every day so all of my affections can be pointed toward you. I want your perspective on everything that touches my life. That is the gold I want to pursue over everything else. Amen

GOD IS IN CONTROL

DAY 6

"We humans keep brainstorming options and plans,
but God's purpose prevails."

PROVERBS 19:21 THE MESSAGE

No matter what things look like. No matter how you feel. No matter what others tell you. One thing remains constant. God is in control. And our acceptance of that truth, well, it determines our enjoyment of the "ride" as He gets us to our "destination". But chances are, if you're human, the subject of SOVEREIGNTY is going to challenge you at some point in your journey here on Earth.

SOVEREIGNTY: the right and power to command, decide, rule or judge; complete authority in a situation; total jurisdiction; absolute dominion; one's rightful prerogative

A few years ago, I went on a cruise with a group of friends and our spouses to celebrate our 50th birthdays. Our itinerary included seven days of traveling to five different islands. When we boarded our ship, we placed our trust in the captain and his route for our journey—and away we sailed to uncharted territories! But while on our trip, what if I was to get concerned and go to the captain and explain to him that I couldn't see "land" or complain that it was "dark" and I couldn't see where we were going? What do you think his response would be to me? I don't know about you, but this is what I would imagine he'd say: "Mrs. Kirkindoll. You can trust me. I have sailed a ship or two before. I know where we're going. I just need you to sit back and enjoy the ride."

To the captain, that would be and should be an acceptable answer. But what if my response was this: "Well, that's not a good enough answer! I need to see some evidence of land—right now! I need to see your entire road map and I need you to shine a giant spotlight out onto the water so I will be able to see anything and everything that might be coming our way!!" And then, picture this conversation not being the end of it. Every time my anxious thoughts got the best of me, I went back and protested again. And again. Banging with everything I had out of frustration on the glass that separated me, as a passenger, from his work area—with me, becoming more and more exasperated and disgruntled with every encounter I had with him.

What do you think his response would be at that point? Probably, the first thing he would say is: "SECURITY, please!!" (And rightfully so!!) But do you think he would feel obligated to honor my request? And moreover, do you think by not honoring my request that it meant he was uncaring or that he didn't really know what he was doing? To the contrary, he might respond like this: "Listen, Mrs. Kirkindoll. I see that you have become anxious about this leg of the journey. But I need you to know that I know what I'm doing. I need you to trust me and enjoy the things that you know have been provided for your pleasure and benefit on this trip—and believe that you will arrive to your final destination safely. It's my job to get you there and you can trust that I'll do that. If you start to get nervous, remember what I've assured you of. Otherwise, sit back and enjoy the ride." Sounds like a more than reasonable response... especially if he has refrained from the temptation to throw me overboard at this point!

We can laugh at the thought of this conversation. But I do believe there is a powerful lesson here. If we can understand the ridiculousness of this regarding a human's capabilities and knowledge, how much more ridiculous are we being about an ALL POWERFUL—ALL KNOWING—COMPLETELY SOVEREIGN GOD?? Please understand this. Being able to control everything that touches your life is a myth. And our constant NEED to control it all, well it's the greatest robber EVER of God's peace in our day-to-day lives.

You have The Great Navigator at the helm of your journey. I say this with tears in my eyes as I type out these words because I know from personal experience how hard it can be to apply these truths. Trusting God when the trip has been long, the waves have been rough, and there is no "land" in sight...is not for the faint of heart. But one thing is certain. Our stories, these stories of trust and resolve to honor Christ while in uncharted territory, these my friends will be stories worth telling when we get to the other side. We will look back and see that "The Wind" was at our backs the whole time...and so will everybody that's looking on. The snapshots of our journeys will be reminders of His goodness and testimonies of faith that will draw others to trust God too. So, don't panic and jump overboard. Taking matters into your own hands, because you have decided God doesn't know what He's doing, only exhausts you and leaves you treading water instead of making steady progress. Instead, set your heart on "cruise". Believe God loves you. Do what you know to do—then trust The Captain with the rest. And with every ounce of faith you've got, CHOOSE to enjoy the ride.

Lord, I confess that I have fallen for the lie that 'I have control of things' way too many times. Help me to look at your Sovereignty as a gift rather than resent the fact that I don't get to be in control. Only the enemy of my soul would want to see me robbed of the gold treasure that comes from trusting you when I can't see what is ahead. Give me the supernatural grace to enjoy the ride even though the waves are rocking my boat. You, Father God, CAN BE TRUSTED. Help me stay focused on that truth today. Amen

MARKERS

DAY 7

"When all the people had crossed the Jordan, the LORD said to Joshua, "Now choose twelve men, one from each tribe. Tell them, 'Take twelve stones from the very place where the priests are standing in the middle of the Jordan. Carry them out and pile them up at the place where you will camp tonight." So, Joshua called together the twelve men he had chosen—one from each of the tribes of Israel. He told them, "Go into the middle of the Jordan, in front of the Ark of the LORD your God. Each of you must pick up one stone and carry it out on your shoulder—twelve stones in all, one for each of the twelve tribes of Israel. We will use these stones to build a memorial. In the future your children will ask you, 'What do these stones mean?' Then you can tell them, 'They remind us that the Jordan River stopped flowing when the Ark of the LORD's Covenant went across.' These stones will stand as a memorial among the people of Israel forever." So the men did as Joshua had commanded them. They took twelve stones from the middle of the Jordan River, one for each tribe, just as the LORD had told Joshua. They carried them to the place where they camped for the night and constructed the memorial there. Joshua also set up another pile of twelve stones in the middle of

the Jordan, at the place where the priests who carried the Ark of
the Covenant were standing.
And they are there to this day."

Joshua 4:1-9 NLT

I'm so moved by this passage of scripture in God's Word. It always takes me back to the summer I first studied it in depth. It actually stirs me to the point of tears as I write because I will never forget the circumstances happening in our lives when I was studying it. We had been praying and waiting for the Lord to give us direction on something specific in our lives for months and He had just miraculously moved on our behalf. In fact, when our prayers were answered, they were done with such stunning confirmation that we could not deny the hand of God within it.

Have you ever had God answer a prayer for you like that? Have you ever seen His hand in something—and it was undeniable that He was orchestrating an outcome? Maybe it was the birth of a baby. Maybe the restoration of a marriage. Maybe it was a long-awaited soul mate finally entering or reentering your life. Or maybe it was as simple as meeting a need such as a rent payment in a month when there seemed to be no way it could be done. But God did it.

Do you realize why the Lord asked Joshua to instruct the people to make a memorial in honor of this particular miracle? So that they would never forget. And, why was this so important? Because although they had seen God work a miracle, it would not be long until difficulty and doubt would cause them to question the goodness of God—again. They needed to be reminded that He is with them. Their children's children needed to hear the stories of God's faithfulness so when despair knocked on their doors, they would know that God has made a way for them before and that He will do it again.

My encouragement today is simple: Be sure to make a memorial in honor of the miraculous ways God moves in your life. Whether you do something as simple as starting a rock garden by writing the miracles and the dates that God moves on your behalf on smooth stones or framing a special photograph that marks a significant event—just be sure to have a place you can easily refer back to as a reminder of His provision. A special figurine, a framed note or a key mounted in a significant place can all be instant reminders of His faithfulness. Only you will know what that notable item should be. But the important thing is to be sure to strategically place these visual markers as beautiful tributes, storytellers and reminders for all who come across them in the years to come.

One of our markers is hanging on our wall. It happens to be a painting that we cherish. It's become one of the dearest things we own. We can hang it right side up or upside down. We choose to hang it upside down. To a new observer, it looks like an artsy fartsy mess. To them, it's just an abstract painting. But we know those blobs of color represent something far more powerful. You see, an artist friend of mine gave me the painting. It was a representation of the piece he painted at one of my events. The painting was actually painted "upside down", though no one knew that at the time. But to everyone's amazement looking on, when he finished the painting, he turned it right side up and it became a stunning picture of Jesus. The gasps in the room were profound—and the same reaction continues to take place in our home when we share its hidden treasure with others. And what makes it truly uncanny—every time—is how Jesus's face can't be seen in it by anyone until you turn it around.

There is a stunning truth for all of us in this story today. When everything is a mess, sometimes we can't see Jesus in it. But once He turns things around, His face within the "chaos" cannot be denied. In fact, if you look at our painting, once you have seen His face, even when it's upside down, you can't "un-see" it anymore. No matter what angle you look at it, you can see His face. For our family, this painting is a reminder that no matter how things look, Jesus is with us. When I look at it to this day, I feel Him whisper in my ear, "LeeAnn, never forget, I'm in it. Don't look at the chaos, keep looking for me. You will see Me in all of it one day."

Why does it continue to be such a powerful reminder? Because we had an experience with Him that we can never "unknow" again. The painting is our reminder to this day. It is now a staple in our home. A marker of God's faithfulness, for not only us, but for all who enter our home and hear the powerful story behind it. How are you displaying the evidence of God's GOLD in your life? What are the physical reminders that tell others the story of His faithfulness?

Lord, thank you that Your faithfulness is not dependent upon mine. Prompt me to hold close the memories of Your goodness. I want professions of Your faithfulness to be in my line of sight on a daily basis. I desire that gratitude consistently fall from my lips, instead of despair, when times are challenging. What a privilege it is to be loved by such a great God. May Your praises be lifted high and Your miraculous works be remembered forever and ever. Amen

DAY 8

*"For it is God who works in you, both to will
and to work for his good pleasure."*

PHILIPPIANS 2:13 KJV

Okay. Can we take a sec to talk about these shoes? And can we just go ahead and get something out on the table—I actually own a pair of these shoes. And before you even get the question out of your mouth, the answer is "yes". They do make my heart skip a beat. However, I must admit, they are EXTRA. For sure. But I do LOVE that they help drive home the point of today's focus.

Let's "walk into each day" with the word EXTRA on our mind. More specifically, what's something EXTRA we can do for someone else? Maybe for our spouse? For a friend? For a family member? Possibly even a perfect stranger?

And what might EXTRA look like? Oh, I'm so glad you asked!! There are an infinite number of ways we can go out of our way and do EXTRA each day!

Buy someone's coffee who isn't expecting it!
Send someone flowers just because you want to bless them!

Give a genuine compliment or word of affirmation to a stranger! Make a
double batch of something yummy and give it to a neighbor!
Buy a bag of groceries and donate it to your local food bank or shelter!
Serve someone breakfast in bed! Give someone preference in line! Pass
on your books, wrapped in beautiful ribbon after you've read them,
for someone else to enjoy!
Drag your neighbor's empty trash cans back up the driveway!
Maybe it's as simple as inviting and treating someone to dinner!
Or, maybe it's as huge as 'gifting' a car to someone in need!

Everyone's "EXTRA" will look a little different based on the resources
they have been blessed with. But let's make it a point to do more than
necessary today—and every day moving forward. Ask the Lord each
morning to point out people who you can bless on His behalf. Let's start
allowing EXTRA to become second nature in our everyday lives.

And for good measure, why don't you try a pair of those gold tennis
shoes on yourself while you're at it? After all, those 'sparkly and comfy
spectacles' were made for walking...and SHINING...and to go around
doing good! Let's wear them with confidence and make a GOLDEN
impression on someone who needs to see evidence of the favor our
Heavenly Father desires to give anyone in our path.

*Heavenly Father, my prayer is simple today: Send me people
to bless. Inspire me with caring ideas that will show others just
how shiny Your love is. Help me to discern every opportunity
wherein I can be Your hands and feet. I'm realizing more every
day that my life is not my own and neither are my resources.
Everything I have is at Your disposal: my assets, my time and
my creativity. I can't wait to see what You have me doing for
others this week! May my attitude on giving always reflect Your
attitude on giving. That's the way to leave a lasting impression
on others that truly is the purest of gold. Amen*

TRANSFORMATION

DAY 9

"Do not be conformed to this world, but be transformed by the renewal of your mind, that by testing you may discern what is the will of God, what is good and acceptable and perfect."

ROMANS 12:2 ESV

When I first saw this picture, I almost passed right by it. The whole transformation analogy using butterflies has been taught so much, I didn't see the reason for doing it again. But this picture, well, it wouldn't let me go with just a quick glance. I sensed a deeper lesson for you and me as I looked intently at these delicate miracles...and I think you will agree.

I decided to look up the transformation process of a butterfly. I was genuinely surprised at what I learned. The caterpillar doesn't just lay in the cocoon until it magically becomes a butterfly. During the transformation process, a small opening appears in the cocoon. For the next several hours, it will struggle to force its body through that little hole. The small pinpoint of light provided by that tiny opening is what the new butterfly uses as a guide to reach its final destination. But what I didn't realize is that this tiny caterpillar is in for the fight of its life! The journey through that tiny opening, though it be extremely hard, is God's way of forcing fluid from the body of the butterfly into its wings so it will be ready for flight once it achieves its freedom from the cocoon. To be an onlooker, the process seems hopeless. One might think the butterfly WON'T make it out. It may even die in the process. But with focus and determination—literally by just following through on what it's designed to do—it not only emerges, but it FLIES like it's floating and delights us with its beautiful colors. The transformation process which may have seemed brutal in technique had not only a miraculous outcome but a stunning one as well.

Let's take some cues from the butterfly's playbook. It knows what to do and doesn't give up until the final transformation is complete. It doesn't sit on the information it has and not apply it to the actual trans-formation process—yet still expect the BEAUTIFUL RESULTS promised by God. When God reveals new things to you in His Word, you have to apply it to gain freedom in your life. He gives you INFORMATION for the purpose of TRANSFORMATION. He doesn't want you to give up when it gets hard. He wants you to keep your eyes on THE LIGHT and fight through until the transforming work is done. He knows that the challenging circumstances you are in are producing strength, character and wisdom that will in turn be a vital part of living out your unique purpose. Trust that He knows not only what you need, but that He has a beautiful result in mind. It's all about perseverance and trusting God throughout the process.

I have a newfound respect for the butterfly. They may look "delicate", but they are far from it. They're not wimps. So, let's not be either. Even if it's just a pinpoint, keep your eye on the light. Keep pushing forward. Because friend, you're about to get your GOLD wings.

Father, this transforming work You are doing in me is exhausting at times. I truly just want to give up when things get too hard. But today, I pray that my perseverance game would kick up a notch. I ask you to keep my eyes focused on the light that you are moving me toward. I don't want to gain information each week through bible study and church—yet never apply it to my life where it can do it's transforming work. Thank you that my end result will be stunning. Give me a mindset that trusts you in this refining process. I can't wait to emerge as GOLD. Amen

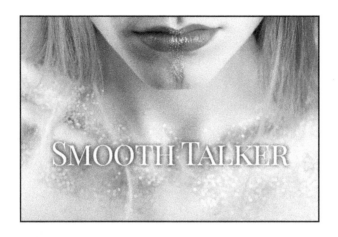

SMOOTH TALKER

DAY 10

"No temptation has overtaken you but such as is common to man;
and God is faithful, who will not allow you to be tempted beyond
what you are able, but with the temptation will provide the way of
escape also, so that you will be able to endure it."

1 CORINTHIANS 10:13 NASB

Have you ever met a smooth talker? You know the kind of person I'm talking about. They are the ones who get another person to do their bidding by using a slick, gently persuasive or seductive manner. A smooth-talking person communicates very confidently. They speak in a way that is likely to persuade people, but they may not be sincere or honest. Smooth talkers are usually personified as "con men" who get what they want from you and then leave a destructive wreckage behind for you to deal with. Most of the time, none of us see them coming—unless you've been burned by one of these smooth talkers a time or two in the past.

Whether you realize it or not, you are more than likely interacting with a smooth talker on a daily basis. She goes by the name, TEMPTATION—and she is a weapon used *consistently* by the enemy of your soul. Her greatest disguise is her 'hint of gold' that tends to distract you from seeing who she really is. I have been suckered by her so many times in life—almost to the point that it's embarrassing to admit. But I will say this, I'm getting a little wiser to her slick schemes and finding that the Bible has longed to teach us about her, if only we'd pay attention.

So how can we be smarter at recognizing temptation when she comes knocking on our door? How can we shut down that smooth talker before she ever gets started? Let's start by taking a look at her qualities.

Temptation preys upon the weak-minded who don't have a plan or resolve.

Temptation is always alluring. I've heard it said that if "your sin" isn't enjoyable at the time, you aren't "doing it right". (Sorry, but it's true.)

Temptation always invites you to take part. She doesn't come with a "warning label".

Temptation has no subtlety— even though she sometimes speaks with a whisper.

Temptation is prepared to do its work. She knows what you like and makes your participation convenient—right at your disposal.

Temptation is talkative. In fact, she desires to do "all of the talking". She will cunningly answer our objections before we even get a chance to protest.

Temptation is usually undercover. She 'tells' you it can stay a secret. However, she always ends up 'telling on you' in the end.

Temptation always leads to an eventual trap.

So now that we recognize her, how do we deal with her? The Bible says in Proverbs that Temptation goes after the simple-minded. And nobody wants that reputation! So that tells me we need the truth of God's Word so deep in our psyche that we recognize her destructive qualities as our number one defense. And right behind that—we need a PRACTICAL PLAN!

For starters, I have found this principle to be the most efficient and successful way to resist temptation: If you don't want to cross the line in a situation, then stay as far away from the line as possible. Standing near the edge—and even entertaining an idea—is usually your eventual first step over the line. Another good line of defense: Don't let her do all the talking! Don't sit there and be passive. Don't let her boss you around! Interrupt that smooth talker with God's Word. Call her out for what she is. And whatever you do, don't linger and listen! Don't allow her to put you in a place to start "considering your options." It just confuses your resolve. And lastly, don't let enjoyment of that temptation be the determining factor!! It will always feel good at "the moment". Never be deceived. It's the moments that come after "that moment" that should be your guide to safety.

The enemy of our hearts preys upon people who "don't know where they are going." If you are wandering around with no plan to be wise, be fully aware that this enemy definitely has a plan for you—and Temptation is his silver bullet. If wisdom is not your guide, "all at once", you can find yourself in a situation you will later wish you would have avoided. So, get smart. Be prepared to recognize this smooth talker when you see her. Temptation can be powerful, but she's not ALL POWERFUL like OUR GOD—who will provide a way of escape from any trap she sets. Yeah, that Temptation, she's no more than a big, fat motor-mouth. But, hey! Her chattering is nothing that a good GOLD muzzle can't take care of, right? Yep, now we're getting somewhere.

Father, when temptation comes, help me to remember these principles. Give me the prompt reminders I need to escape the traps that have been set for me. May I have the wisdom to recognize when I'm in danger of not choosing Your best. Thank you for equipping me with the power to withstand anything that rises against Your amazing plans for my life. I want to live life fancy free—because I'm bondage free. Amen

DAY 11

"May the God of hope FILL YOU with all joy and peace in believing, so that by the power of the Holy Spirit you may abound in hope."

ROMANS 15:13 ESV

Have you ever wanted to make this statement—maybe even shout it from the rooftop: "I have nothing left to give!!!" Yeah, me too. But may I share a little wisdom that was given to me over 20 years ago? It's one of those lessons that has been a good litmus test when I start feeling off balance, frustrated—or for lack of a better word—EMPTY inside. It actually comes in the form of a question. Who's filling your cup?

That may sound like an odd question. But stick with me for a moment. We were created with an emotional 'hole' deep within our souls that longs to be filled by something in order for us to feel 'whole'. Processing the need to be filled is no different than understanding the concept of a cup being created to do the same. No matter *how* we allow "our cup" to be filled—whether it be through attention, success, control, affirmation, or instant gratifications like food or sex—we are miserable until SOMETHING is in it.

But what if we quit looking for the things of this world to fill us and started our days by asking God to fill our cups? (And I mean before our feet ever come over the side of our beds and onto the floor! Right??) Truth is, the beautiful Beth Moore taught me years ago that "He is the ONLY ONE who is never overwhelmed by the depth of our need." Think of it this way. If our "cups" are filled by Him every day FIRST, then any sweet affirmations from a spouse, a child, a friend or a boss would just be an overflow from a cup that's already full. I have found personally that when I follow this practice, I never seem to lack for affection or attention because I'm not dragging others down with the weight of my neediness.

What about you? Do you need to let someone off the hook today? Are you expecting someone or something to take the place of what only God has the power to do in your heart and mind? We choose our "full". So, make the choice to be 'FULL-FILLED' by Christ. That is what actually makes our "insides" GOLD. In fact, let's get our empty cups so full of Him that when someone goes to hug us, our GOLD 'spills' all over them.

Heavenly Father, I confess that many days I have been trying to live out my faith with an empty cup. If I plan on giving away the gold you have given me, I definitely need more of YOU. Thank you for the reminder that no one and nothing else can fill my cup completely like You do. Help me to remember, every day, where my "full" comes from. Amen

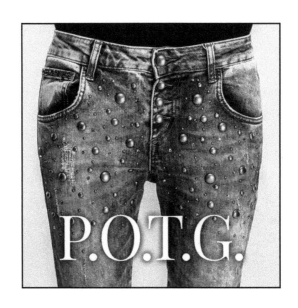

DAY 12

"Therefore confess your sins to each other and pray for each other
so that you may be healed. The prayer of a
righteous person is powerful and effective."

JAMES 5:16 NIV

One January evening several years ago, I randomly got a text from my sister that read: "Pants on the ground! Pants on the ground!" When I read it, for some reason, I immediately believed something was wrong. In my defense, I thought by saying "pants on the ground!", WITH an exclamation point AND repeating it twice, she was telling me to get on my knees RIGHT THAT MINUTE and pray! So, I did.

While praying, I thought, "This isn't enough in this moment. I have to call her and make sure she's ok!" So breathlessly, I scrolled for her number and made the call. When she answered the phone I immediately said, "Oh my gosh, are you ok??" She calmly answered: "Yes. I'm fine. Why do you ask? What's wrong, LeeAnn!?" Of course, at that point, I'm feeling bewildered and say, "Well, YOU just texted ME and said 'pants on the ground'. Soooo, I fell to my knees and started praying!" Next thing I know, I can hear her begin laughing uncontrollably. After a few moments of my dead silence and her continuous belly-laughing, she managed to get out the question: "Have you not watched our favorite singing competition yet?" My response was an emphatic "No!"—followed with an obvious "Why?" Then she began belting the words, 'pants on the ground' as if she were singing a song. Y'all, I was like, "What???? Are you kidding me? I thought you were telling me to literally get my 'pants on the ground'—as if begging me to get my 'knees on the floor' right that second—because your need for prayer was so dire!"

We laughed all night. But let me tell you what was born out of that ridiculous story. We decided that IN REALITY, we should have a "code" we can text when we actually DO need prayer. One, that if sent to us, we'd know to intercede on their behalf with no questions asked. Because sometimes, we can't talk, explain or maybe even admit what's needed in that moment. BUT, we're wise enough to know when we're holding on by a thread. TO THIS DAY, if one of us texts POTG to the other, we know exactly what to do. No questions asked.

Do you have a partner like that? If not, I encourage you to get one and come up with your own 911 prayer code. It's a POWERFUL ACT OF LOVE as well as an HONOR TO PRAY FOR EACH OTHER! So, don't take this encouragement lightly. Get your partner nailed down today. If you already have a precious prayer warrior on speed dial, then take a moment and let her know how much you appreciate her. And girl, while we're at it, let's all get a pair of these 'metallic gold-kissed' jeans to wear while we pray! I hear they're 'one size fits all'. Fabulous, right?? We'd defi-nitely have some SOLID GOLD prayers going up when our knees hit the ground in a pair of those beauties!

Heavenly Father, thank you for laughter. Thank you for life lessons that change the way we manage our everyday lives. I praise you for lining up special prayer partners—just for me and me for them—long before I even knew them. May we always be spiritual warriors on each other's behalf. Give us a deep sense of discernment on how to intercede for each other with prayers that are truly powerful and effective. Bind us together in ways only You can do so that Your Glory will be revealed here on earth as it is in heaven. Amen

FIGHTER

DAY 13

"Yet, I am always with you. You hold me by my right hand."

PSALM 73:23 NIV

S ometimes when I jump into God's Word, I am comforted. Sometimes I get confused. Sometimes I get intrigued. And other times, I get a revelation that just makes me want to get up and sing a fight song. You know what I'm talking about? The kind that gets your blood pumping— like when an athlete has been knocked down one too many times—and now this time, nothing can stop her. The lyrics push you forward, the beat gets your adrenaline flowing and the belief that you have what you need to push through and be victorious is now not just a hope—it's a reality waiting to happen. You probably have a song in your head at this moment. (I had a whole playlist of songs go off in my head after I did my Word by Word study of our verse today!) You'll get a chance to 'feel the beat' your-self when you have some time with this particular verse. But I would love to kick-start your studying with a little 'background music" to enhance your understanding of God's devotion to you.

After some study time in 2 Corinthians, I learned a little behind the scenes information about 'weapons of righteousness' and the significance of them being used specifically in the right or left hands. This information fell fresh again as I was reading through the Psalms. Weapons for the right hand are offensive weapons. Weapons for the left hand are considered defensive weapons. A commentary from Bible Hub went on to say this: "... But it's meaning is sufficiently obvious: The Weapon on the right hand is the sword of the Spirit (Eph 6:17, NIV)—aggressive in conflict with evil. The armor for the left hand is defensive, the shield of faith, which is our defense against the flaming arrows of the evil one (Eph 6:16, NIV). Don't let the significance of this get lost on you. As you read Psalm 73:23 again, try and get a mental picture of what you are reading. Honestly, for me, it's like a GOLD RUSH—too much to contain!

By God taking our right hand, He has taken the hand that is furthest from our heart, as to keep it as far away from harm as possible as He sets out to protect us. We can better understand the significance of this when we remember that the left hand is for defensive weapons. The thought that His mighty left hand is defending my heart and yours from the adversary who would desire to pierce it with his lies and fiery darts strengthens my resolve. But with the picture of His left hand grasped in our right, it should not get by us that God's mighty right hand remains free to fight for us! Remember, the weapon on the right hand is the sword of the spirit fighting aggressively in conflict with evil. Yes! You are seeing—this is no wimpy verse. He is always with us—His mighty left hand of defense in our right hand as HIS MIGHTY RIGHT HAND goes before us to fight our battles. It's an overwhelming picture when you close your eyes and meditate on it.

What is happening in your life as you read this? Are you feeling like your strength is not enough today? Has your head bowed down in defeat over circumstances you fear you can't overcome? I pray today that you feel God gripping your right hand. I hope you hear the thump of a good fight song driving your resolve as you think of God showing up like you've never experienced before. His Word is filled with promises He keeps. He never, ever, ever leaves your side. He's got way more than just your back—It's way better than that. You actually get to hide behind Him as He leads the fight. When your mind is 'battling' thoughts that want to overwhelm you, remember that He is in front of you WINNING THE WAR.

Personally, that makes me want to be brave. His devotion towards me makes me want to be a fighter too. In fact, His ability to defeat the enemy makes me that much stronger. Makes me work a little bit harder. It makes me that much wiser. Yes, God. Thanks for making me a FIGHTER! Oops, I may have just given my "not today, Satan" fight song away! As your personal cheerleader, my word for you is this: Go! Fight! Win! Rise up and face the days ahead with confidence. His hand is in your hand right now. Give it a little squeeze to signify you're in. Why? Because, our God will never stop fighting for you and me.

Wow, what a God. You are mighty! You are worthy of your Name! Thank you for never leaving me or forsaking me—even though I don't show you that same devotion each day. I'm in awe to know that I could have no greater ally as I face my current challenges. Thank you for keeping me in your grip. May you be glorified in my life today. Amen

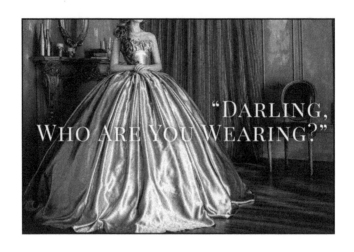

"DARLING, WHO ARE YOU WEARING?"

DAY 14

But the fruit of the Spirit is love, joy, peace, patience, kindness,
goodness, faithfulness, gentleness, and self-control.

GALATIANS 5:22-23A NLT

I won a contest my Senior year in High School. One of the major TV networks had a Fantasy Contest in our viewing area through one of the locally affiliated stations. People of all ages and from all over the region sent in their fantasies. They picked certain entries with the intent of bringing that "fantasy" to life. I sent in a request for the perfect prom night. And yes, yours truly won. When I received the call that I was one of the winners, it was the talk of the town for a few weeks. Of course, the biggest buzz revolved around the question, 'what are you going to wear that night?'. The network crew came through with a custom-made Mike Benet` gown that rivaled any wedding dress at that time. I remember feeling like Cinderella in it. I still recall all of the fittings, the buzz and the TV cameras that were involved in capturing the details leading up to the big night. Yep, I got to have a red carpet moment—and be a starlet for a night. Great memories to last a lifetime, for sure.

But looking back on all that fuss, I can't help but think about where we are as women today. Hollywood has done a good job of convincing us that our outer appearance needs to be "red carpet" ready to be remembered. Put your time into hair appointments, nail appointments, spa treatments and the like. Spend your money on the best clothes, the finest makeup along with fabulous bags and shoes to match if you want to impress people in your spheres of influence. While not one of those things are bad in and of themselves (because you will never hear me shoot down anyone for wearing a fabulous pair of shoes), we can sometimes be tricked into putting all of our energy into our outer shell, while failing to realize our insides need some serious overhauling if we really want to leave a lasting impression that reflects something much more important than ourselves. Take a look at the following definitions. They're the attributes of the Fruit of the Spirit in our scripture focus today.

Love: An affection for others
Joy: An exuberance about life
Peace: Serenity that has a calming effect within and on others
Patience: A willingness to stick with things
Kindness: A sense of compassion deep in our hearts
Goodness: A conviction and holiness that blesses people
Faithfulness: Means finding ourselves in loyal commitments
Gentleness: Not needing to force our way in life
Self-control: Able to direct and guide our energies wisely

Notice anything interesting? Every one of these qualities that are so important to the Lord deal with our inner beauty. We seem to always make time for the 'outer detail' appointments. However, not showing up for our appointments with the Lord to do a little 'inside work' are treated as no biggie. In fact, at the end of our lives, if we aren't more intentional, will our greatest legacy left behind in life be our chic haircuts, our designer clothes or how great our nails looked? That may sound trivial to you, but go with me here for a minute. Just like a woman would choose the exact look she wants to portray on the red carpet, we must do the same in our ordinary "shag carpet" days. If we want what's on the inside to be the showstopper, then we need to consult with 'the designer of our souls' to get the proper pattern for some better fitting 'underwear'—and then SHOW UP to the appointment. I love to think about what the conversations about us would be like if we did.

"Wow, that girl wears LOVE more beautifully than anyone I know. When she entered the room, girl, her JOY lit up the space like a metallic gold taffeta evening dress—it was that eye-catching!" "I know!! And did you watch as she mingled with the crowd? God's undeniable PEACE followed her every step as gracefully as a long train follows a bridal gown. Oh, and speaking of every step she took—she rocked those stilettos of SELF-CONTROL like a boss! She took seriously that the stakes within her encounters were as high as her heels!" Oh! And did you see how PATIENCE held her bodice, the very heart of her, taunt and together more beautifully than the satin ribbon lacing up the back of her gorgeous gown?" "Well, I was simply taken aback by the KINDNESS that fell from her lips. It was more stunning than any shade of pink lipstick in the Chanel makeup line." "Well, personally, I was mesmerized by her GOODNESS. It sparkled like the loveliest of diamond bracelets. It was impressive and could be seen by everyone that her hands reached out to greet. And her FAITHFULNESS—girrrrrrl! It was nothing short of regal! It adorned her head like the sweetest of tiaras...it was obvious she was royalty...a precious Daughter of the King."

When THAT woman enters the room, she literally shines from within...and why? Because she knew that in every room she entered, someone needed to see Jesus—not her. They needed to see her "underwear", not her "outerwear". She knew her "money card" was her "FRUIT" of the looms. Her time was spent on the stuff no one could see on the outside. Instead, what people noticed was the beautiful result of all the "behind the scenes" appointments with God to examine her heart. They experienced firsthand the choices she made to eliminate the distractions that wanted to steal her affections. The intentionality to reflect Christ was displayed in every interaction she had. Why? She knew it was the only way to leave a lasting impression that would honor God and inspire others to do the same.

When we as women of God walk into a room, I want it to be obvious "who we are wearing". I want them to take one look and say—"Whoa, she is wearing the righteousness of Jesus Christ. And she is stunning!! She literally shines! I WANT THAT SAME LOOK!" I want to have faith like hers. I want to have patience like that. I would do anything to experience her joy." And that, my sweet friend, is when you stroll across the 'shag carpet' of your everyday life and take her hand and say, "Come on. Follow me. I can show you exactly where to 'get the look' that SHINES LIKE GOLD."

Lord, I thank you for the many extravagant blessings I get to enjoy. But I pray that there is never any appointment in my books that outranks a standing appointment with You. Help me to embrace the shag carpet moments in my life with the kind of preparation I might spend for a red carpet reveal. You are worthy of all the attention—all of the time. I pray that when others see me each day, they are really getting a glimpse of You. Amen

DAY 15

"We can rejoice, too, when we run into problems and trials, for we know that they are good for us—they help us learn to be patient. And patience develops strength of character in us and helps us trust God more each time we use it until finally our hope and faith are strong and steady. Then, when that happens, we are able to hold our heads high no matter what happens and know that all is well, for we know how dearly God loves us"

ROMANS 5:3-5 TLB

Have you ever felt inspired to start a project, launch a ministry or chase a dream? And I mean the kind of spark where you can't sleep that night because you feel so strongly that God has given you something really special to accomplish! You start making your lists and checking them twice. You might even call a close friend and share your excitement. In your heart and mind, you're convinced that nothing can dull the sparkle of the "ball" you are about to run with.

But lo and behold, despite all of your very best intentions, here come the distractions and challenges. You realize very quickly that the nights are going to get long and there aren't enough hours in your day. So many things need your attention. And on top of that, your family is hungry EVERY.

SINGLE. NIGHT. So, there's grocery shopping to do and meals to be prepared. And we all know that laundry is never going to do itself. And neither are those dishes! So, we put off chasing that project or dream until tomorrow. But now, tomorrow isn't looking much better. Our thoughts move from excitement to thinking, "This is going to be too hard. Maybe this wasn't a good idea. This must be a sign I'm not supposed to do this after all."

But can I share something the Lord is teaching me? Just because it's hard, doesn't mean it's not right. Giving up isn't the answer. Instead, chipping away—a little every day—is the key. A friend of mine made a statement in one of her social media posts that I loved.

"The results are not up to us, but the obedience is."

-Becky Leach

So, if your original "giddy up" is trying to "lay back down", ask the Lord to rekindle your excitement and help you implement a plan to persevere. Embrace the building of your character instead of fighting it. But whatever you do, don't quit. Don't drop that "sparkly GOLD ball". When you do finally reach your goal, you are going to want that baby 'spinning above your head' while you do your HAPPY DANCE at the finish line. And hey...by sticking to your plans in spite of the challenges, well that just might be inspiring someone else along the way to do the same thing. That's 24k living at its finest.

Heavenly Father, You say that you know the plans you have for me. You also promise that if you call us to it that you will see us through it. Lord, please help me to not give up when things get hard. Instill the kind of character in me that will thrive on doing hard things instead of shying away from them. Build perseverance in me that proves your faithfulness to others. May the refinement of these challenges emerge as nothing short of pure gold when the finished product is revealed for the world to see. Amen

REACH FOR THE SKY

DAY 16

"My mouth is filled with your praise, declaring
your splendor all day long."

PSALM 71:8 NIV

Do you find it hard to give God your undivided attention? If we are getting real here, most of the times I sit down to spend time quietly in His presence, my mind is anything but quiet. I don't know about you, but ideas run through my mind at mach speed! And no matter how much work I have done to be ready to focus—like having my Bible, pens, journal, highlighter and COFFEE all at hand—it seems that anytime I choose to spend time with the Lord, I will invariably think of a million things I can't forget to do. I'll remember I have a load of laundry that needs to be done. I'll suddenly have guilt over not unloading the dishwasher...but seem to be fine with it any other time! Ugh! You too? And to make matters even more complicated, I tend to add to the chaos of my supposed "quiet time" by doing all of the talking: praying for family, voicing our needs, giving Him my concerns and asking one question after another because I have convinced myself that I am on a "need to know" basis with God—which is an issue that needs addressing as well. Anyone else relating here?

Frustrated with the whole process one morning and feeling like my prayers were hitting the ceiling and boomeranging back to mock all of my efforts, I begged the Lord to help me. He mercifully prompted me to turn on a worship playlist and then I closed my eyes. In the wee hours of that morning, I quieted everything but the praise in my heart as I focused on EVERY WORD that was being sung. I relished in the truth of who God is. I internalized every reminder of His love for me. I marveled at every wonder held gently by His majesty. Yes. God WANTS to hear from us. He desires communication with His children. But we were also CREATED to give praise where praise is due—FIRST.

We spend so much time trying to bring God DOWN to our level in order to make sense of all that is happening in this world. But there is a powerful shift in our weary, busy, broken, conflicted, and self-absorbed hearts when our hands lift to the sky in worship. What a sweet release it is when we reach UP toward His level of understanding instead. That is where the GOLD is found, my friend. It is so true that when "the praises go up, the blessings come down." So, what do you say? Let's REACH FOR THE SKY today before we do anything else. Let's allow our hearts the privilege of worshiping the Name above all Names—Jesus Christ our King. What a beautiful name it truly is.

Lord, You are worthy of my undivided attention and more than worthy to be praised. Forgive me for tending to making it "all about me" when I come into your presence. Mature me so that I can magnify Your name from a pure heart of gratitude. I want to be second. You deserve to be first. Anytime that order gets mixed up, I pray the Holy Spirit will quickly prompt me to put You back in the place of honor that is yours alone. As I worship You today, I pray it sounds different than it did yesterday—because I want my love for You to grow deeper and deeper with every encounter in your presence. Accept my worship as gold treasure as I raise my hands toward heaven in awe of the beautiful name above all names—Jesus. Amen

DAY 17

"If you've gotten anything at all out of following Christ,
if His love has made any difference in your life, if being in a com-
munity of the Spirit means anything to you, if you have a heart,
if you care—then do me a favor: Agree with each other, love each
other, be deep-spirited...Put yourself aside,
and help others get ahead...Forget yourselves long enough
to help another move forward."
PHIL 2:1-4 *THE MESSAGE*

I'd like to give a sentimental shout out to all the mommas, friends, daughters, granddaughters, daughters-in-law, nieces, mentors and the many other people who have been blessed by them. The disciplined exercise we're discussing today gives us an opportunity to not only BE GOLD...but actually LEAVE GOLD as well.

Of all the many things we do throughout our lifetime for our families, our church members, our co-workers and in some instances those we may never get the opportunity to meet: do not neglect to WRITE DOWN blessings of affirmation to those in your sphere of influence. They could be our children and grandchildren. Maybe our parents, our siblings or our extended family. It could be someone you work with or someone who works for you. That person might be someone you are mentoring each week or someone in a mission field that you have never met. But this I truly believe. There is no one on the planet who doesn't want affirmation of what their life means to another. So, put your love for them—and ultimately God's love for them—down on paper.

Encourage them in their gifts and share lessons that God has taught you along the way. Tell them about the love of Jesus...in your handwriting. Share the prayers you are praying for them behind the scenes. Be purposeful in passing on the legacy of love you pray they'll one day carry. Give these love notes to them now or save some to be lingered over later. But take the time to do it. The days are passing quickly. And one day, we won't be here to share all of the loving words that reside in our hearts. Because of that reality, it's important that we record our thoughts for them to read...and read...and then read again. That gift will be priceless one day. These compilations of love and affirmation will be more valuable than any toy, device or designer bag they will have tossed aside by this time next year.

May I go first by taking a moment to encourage YOU? You are loved and highly favored. You are called to bring light where darkness begs to preside. God has someone in mind—maybe several in mind—who need to "read your heart". Don't withhold that precious gift.

To those of you out there doing the "momma thing", keep going. Stay strong. This labor of love we do is not in vain. Find creative ways to tell your children that they are a unique and cherished unconditionally. To those of you desperately wishing to take on that role but have no evidence of that dream in your arms today, don't lose heart. Write to that sweet child you are longing to meet. Those words have a precious sparkle to them that will guard your heart and your faith as you wait on the Lord. To the many of you caring for people who challenge your resolve to love, ask The Lord how He feels about them and affirm that in writing. It will bring hope to your calling and healing to your heart—and their hearts as well.

Is it your mother? Is it a neighbor? A friend? An anonymous woman who has been marginalized by another in her life and now desperately needs to know that she is valued and cherished in spite of what she has endured? Don't put off what you can do today. Turn off the TV. Maybe put down your cell phone. But pick up the nearest pen...and start writing those 'love letters'. Those special words will truly be SOLID GOLD to the ones who receive it. And you never know. You might just see a chain reaction develop. Hopefully they too will go on to bless another—who will then go on to bless another. And yep, that next one might then go on to bless yet another. Wow! I don't know about you, but I sense a love fest in the making! So, what do you say? Let the first note begin with you—TODAY.

Lord, help me make a list of the people YOU want me to encourage or affirm. Give me the words to express my heart in ways that will be a gift to the person who reads it. Don't allow me to procrastinate when those names come to my mind. Remove any hindrances that would keep me from following through on these important notes. May you be glorified as others are reminded of their value. Make my pen a holy instrument for good. In your name I pray. Amen

SET YOUR GAZE

DAY 18

*"Your eyes are windows into your body. If you open your eyes
wide in wonder and belief, your body fills up with light. If you live
squinty-eyed in greed and distrust, your body is a dark cellar. If
you drop the blinds on your windows, what a dark life you will
have!" "Give your entire attention to what God is doing right now,
and don't get worked up about what may or may not happen
tomorrow. God will help you deal with whatever hard things come
up when the time comes."*

MATT 6:22-23, 34 THE MESSAGE

"Be careful little eyes what you see...". Do you remember the words
to that song? If you grew up attending Sunday School at a local
church, then you grew up singing it. It was most likely one of the first
songs you would learn in any denomination other than "Jesus Loves
Me". It even had hand gestures to help commit the lyrics to memory. We
sang it loud and proud—most likely taking a bow with our friends before
the teacher as we concluded. All the while, unbeknownst to us as small

children, we were being taught a golden litmus test whose worth would turn out to be most valuable later in life.

I've found myself noticing more and more that my outlook on my circumstances is completely in sync with where I set my gaze. If you look up the definition of the word 'gaze', you will find that it means to look steadily, intently, and with fixed attention. What are you keeping your fixed attention on? It's an important question. Because where you set your gaze matters to your heart. Are you 'intently and steadily fixed on' disappointing circumstances? Your unfulfilled wish list? On the argumentative posture of political views? Preoccupied with the lifestyles of reality TV personalities? Maybe hyper-focused on the ever-changing ideas of what the world says will make us happy? All of those things can be breeding grounds for discontentment. Let's take time each day to 'look with fixed attention' upon our many blessings. Let your eyes linger on a passage in God's Word. Allow them to rest on a Holy perspective that not only "enLIGHTens" you but also challenges you to be a distributor of that precious LIGHT.

"The more you focus on The LIGHT of the World, the LIGHTER your load in turn becomes." LK

So be watchful today of where you set your gaze. Be purposeful in what you let your eyes and mind rest on each day. Challenge yourself to live out those lyrics you were taught all those years ago—knowing as you choose to give fixed attention to God's perspective on your current circumstances, you can trust that He loves you and has HIS GOLDEN GAZE locked in on YOU.

Father, I'm so thankful that you will never take your eyes off of me. I ask for your forgiveness because my own eyes tend to focus on other things quite easily. Holy Spirit, will you prompt me to notice when I have my eyes fixed on things that will distract me from focusing on the truth of God's Word? May I be a gold-giver and a distributor of Your light every day. Amen

DAY 19

"You've all been to the stadium and seen the athletes race.
Everyone runs; one wins. Run to win. All good athletes train hard.
They do it for a gold medal that tarnishes and fades. You're after
one that's gold eternally. I don't know about you, but I'm running
hard for the finish line. I'm giving it everything I've got. No sloppy
living for me! I'm staying alert and in top condition. I'm not going
to get caught napping, telling everyone else all about it and then
missing out myself."

1 COR 9:24-27 THE MESSAGE

Comparison. It's become the ultimate dirty word in women's ministry conversations across the country. It's been deemed a courage killer. A confidence thief. It's the contentment-devouring word that no woman wants to see intersect with her destiny. In fact, everywhere you look, someone is addressing it. We see posts on social media, chapters in books and entire Bible studies devoted to the topic. Each of these venues are desperately encouraging us to avoid the trap of comparing our abilities, opportunities and resources against what others have at their disposal. Yet, here we are. Many of us are still stuck at the "starting gate" of a purpose driven life because we can't get our eyes off of everyone else! Stuck in wishing mode. Stuck in feeling sorry for ourselves because we don't have the same opportunities someone else does. Maybe even trying to copy others around us rather than focusing in on the unique ways God wants to use our gifts to make a mark in this world for His glory. And we wonder why our ministry opportunities are falling flat?

With that thought in mind, let me ask you a question. Do you know why race horses wear blinders? They're actually a very simple solution to a common problem for all horses running a race. These amazing animals have peripheral vision that allows them to see a panoramic view of the world. But this gift of unhindered sight can also be a hindrance without a form of protection in place when focus is needed. Blinders cover the rear and side vision of the horse, forcing him to set his eyes in a forward direction. This protects them from becoming distracted or panicked by what they see around them. And why is this so important? Because they have to concentrate on not only running, but making it to the finish line.

So it goes with us. Today, through the World Wide Web, we can see so much happening around us. And although that can inspire and encourage us at times, it can also be a real distraction. We have a RACE TO RUN—and we have been given all that we need in our unique spheres of influence to not only run our race but to FINISH STRONG! I don't know about you, but I'm IN IT TO WIN IT! So, what do you say? Let's line up TOGETHER, with our blinders safely in place, and shoot out of that starting gate with our eyes on the GOLD—the kind that affects someone's eternity. Hey!! I think I just heard a shot fired from the starter's pistol! Better giddy-up, friend! But, hey—before we take off! Don't you think we look marvelous running alongside each other today? Your GOLD sure is shiny! May everything YOU touch be blessed beyond measure! I want you to know that I'm super proud of you and that you're always in my prayers each day.

Heavenly Father, why is it so easy to get distracted and caught up in comparison? Why does it always feel like someone is doing it just a little bit "shinier" than me? Help me to BELIEVE that I am who YOU say I am—and that what you have called me to do is valuable and filled with Kingdom purposes. Thank you for giving me every single thing I need to accomplish the things you have me working on. May I rest in your love for me today and get excited about my future at a level worthy of my calling! Amen

DAY 20

*"...give me neither poverty nor riches! Give me just enough
to satisfy my needs. For if I grow rich, I may deny you
and say, Who is the LORD? And if I am too poor,
I may steal and thus insult God's holy name."*

PROVERBS 30:8B-9 NLT

What drives a steady, day-to-day relationship with the Lord? How can we maintain it? For me, recognizing my tendencies and how they've shaped my habits has been eye-opening. Let's take a moment together and examine our habits through the narratives that follow and the powerful instruction of God's Word.

We have all seen or read many stories that have a "rags to riches" theme. In the last few years, a very popular movie told the story of a young boy who suffered unspeakable loss and was so poor he had to steal to eat. He then sets his mind to change his circumstances and makes an inner vow to never be in that place again. He goes on to acquire great wealth and notoriety only to lose it all—along with his family and his reputation. Why? Because he let what he wanted get in the way of what he really needed. Solomon, noted in the Bible as the wisest man who ever lived, experienced having not only unmatched wisdom but riches and honor as well. Yet, he allowed those blessings to draw his heart and loyalty away from God. In the end, not only was his kingdom compromised, but a curse to destroy that kingdom completely manifested itself during his son's reign—teaching all of us a valuable lesson. Our focus, our ability to manage our blessings, and our diligence to check our loyalties ALL have a lasting effect—not only on us but also on those who our lives directly influence. Both of these stories lead us to ask the question: "How can we balance the tension between being without or having so much that we lose our devotion to God?" I believe the answer is found by, what I call, staying in a "Sweet Spot" with the Lord.

Through the years—more times than I want to admit—the strength of my relationship with God was dictated by the highs and lows in my life. When things were challenging, I was on my knees every day praying, asking for wisdom and seeking to see Him in tangible ways. However, once the crisis was over, my tendency was to get lax in my prayer life again. I wasn't as concerned with what God thought about my everyday choices. Instead of staying in a place of reverence, filled with thanksgiving for answers to prayer, I put my Bible AND God back on a shelf as if I'd forgotten I ever needed either one of them. The urgency to hear from Him seemed to fade into the background of my 'blessed' life. But on the other hand, when a crisis did draw me back to God and I found myself in a place of 'desperation' for too long, I'd be tempted to give up hope and start taking matters into my own hands. My dependence shifted from God onto my abilities and solutions. Both were equally disruptive to our fellowship!

Asking the Lord to keep me in the SWEET SPOT with Him EVERYDAY has been the best way to "keep myself honest" before the Lord. He's shown me how distracted I can become when I'm completely satisfied by my blessings. I'm easily prone to being captivated by them over The Blesser himself. Do you struggle with that too? Ugh!

But also during my time with Him, He has reminded me to simply ask for what I need that day—rather than reciting and begging for all I think I need. It has been a powerful practice to develop! It not only ushers in an opportunity to trust my Heavenly Father with His very best for me but it in turn releases me from placing my hope in the expectation of what I think those answers should look like. So rather than believe the answer is always, "I need MORE"—and assume He didn't care when the answer was "you need LESS"—MY GOAL IS THE SWEET SPOT.

Choosing the discipline of time with The Lord everyday—no matter what is going on in my life—and submitting to what He knows to be best for me, allows me to stay in perfect fellowship with Him. I can enjoy the blessings when they come and still trust Him when times are hard. It's kind of like the satisfaction that comes from eating something sweet and salty. The combo keeps you wanting MORE! Right?? And truthfully, that's what I want. More and more of Christ, showing me that every "spot" I'm in throughout my life can be "sweet" as long as my trust is in Him.

Lord, I don't want to have a feast or famine relationship with You. I want spending time with You to be as important to me as the air I breathe for survival each day. Help me to internalize the fact that you have gone before me and also have come in behind me to ensure that my relationship with you has an opportunity to stay vibrant through any season I'm walking through. I know where my GOLD is found...right in the spot I spent time with You the day before. Amen

SHATTERED

DAY 21

"And I am certain that God, who began the good work within you,
will continue his work until it is finally finished
on the day when Christ Jesus returns."

PHILIPPIANS 1:6 NLT

I was really lucky to grow up having grandparents that were crazy about me. You know what I mean? The kind of grandmothers that think everything you do is precious—to the point they've become convinced that you -most certainly- are 'the smartest child on the planet'. You know the ones. Maybe you had one like that too or you've become that grand-mother yourself at this point in life! My mom taught me tons of nursery rhymes as a toddler and I could recite them flawlessly upon request. My parents lovingly tell of my Nannie being so taken aback by my ability to recall so many that she cautioned my mother to be careful because she may be 'forcing in' too much information 'for my sweet little brain to handle'...oh dear! And though she may have been worried about that for a hot minute, she went on and marveled all the same. Yes, there was one thing I never had to question growing up: I was priceless and valuable in their eyes. And they made sure I knew that.

My Nannie was one of the most caring people you'd ever meet. She was a faith-filled compassionate woman marked by her love for Jesus. I preferred a bowl of her purple hull peas over a bowl of ice cream any day! She was a joyful person with a darling giggle. I personally never heard her complain a day in her life. As a child, I would have had no idea that she had grown up extremely poor. Maybe that contributed to her attitude of gratitude in life, but I can tell you that they had so little, that she emerged from that era of life with only one possession of her mother's—a small ceramic teapot. Because my Nannie was just a young child when her mother passed away, I can only imagine how especially cherished it was. So, the day it shattered into hundreds of pieces, I feel like her heart must have shattered equally along with it. Yes, you read that right. It shattered.

My guess is, you are picturing her right now, sweeping up the pieces as she wiped her tears—swallowing down hard sobs as she poured a dustpan full of shattered pottery into a trash can. But if that is where your thoughts went, you would be wrong. She might have been in tears, but she picked up every single piece from the floor and placed them on the table instead of a trash can. She began to separate them and lay them flat just as someone would prepare to piece together a puzzle. And after weeks of tedious laboring, she successfully glued that teapot back together. *THAT* is how valuable it was to her. And friend, little did she realize in those moments of putting that teapot back together, that her labor of love would be leaving a beautiful analogy for all of us regarding how valuable we are to God.

When things come in and blindside us and seem to leave us shattered, God does not look at us and think, "well, I guess I'm going to have to toss her away." Or, "this situation pushed her way too far past my redemption". Or, "her potential for great impact is now lost because she is far too broken". Instead, His first thought is rescue. His next move is preparation. Then He begins rebuilding. His plan is complete restoration. And He will not give up until it is done. He picks us up from our pile of rubble and begins to strategically place us in a position to be pieced back together again. And just like my precious Nannie, He cherishes you so much that

He will not go halfway and then give up. In His eyes, just as in hers, you are too valuable to stop at anything short of complete restoration.

Most of us will never live up to the perfection a loving grandparent sees in us. But we can live every day of our lives assured that we are priceless and valuable to our Heavenly Father—and that our value drives His never-ending devotion to see us fully restored when life seems to shatter us. Have you believed the lie that your value has somehow been diminished? That you are past the point of being restored? Have you decided another person in your life is past redemption and will never be who they were intended to be? God wants us to know His perspective on these truths. He wants you and me to be assured that the misplaced or shattered pieces of our lives are not bound for some 'spiritual trash can'. They are on His table, ready to be reassembled. Destined to be displayed again for His glory.

I was lucky enough to have that precious teapot passed on to me. When I look at it, I see a symbol of the lengths someone will go to restore something that holds great value to them. It will forever inspire me to do the hard work it takes to mend broken relationships, severed trust and shattered dreams. But more than anything, I want this legacy that my Nannie has passed down to be a reminder that God will never give up on restoring ME. I want to pass that message down to my children and grandchildren—the message that He will never give up on restoring THEM. And the purpose of telling you this story? I want you to read these words and look at this photo and be reminded that God will never give up on restoring YOU. He will rebuild until you're not only pieced back together but you shine like GOLD as well.

Will you let Him get to work on piecing things back together again? Will you let him turn the shattered parts of your life into a reflection of His redemptive GOLD? When He is done, the image you *see* will be more stunning than you ever dreamed—the testimony of His goodness you *share* too beautiful to conceal.

Thanks, Nannie—-from all of us. Your life will always be remembered as one worthy of modeling. If we could enjoy tea with you in this moment, poured from your precious 'mosaic' teapot, our cups would be raised in your honor. Yes, well done, precious one.

Father, I ask that You make a way where there seems to be no way today. Please restore and rebuild the broken things in my life and in the lives of my loved ones too. Thank you that I can be assured that help is on the way and that nothing is beyond repair when it is placed in Your hands. Above all, may you be glorified in the restoration. Amen

DAY 22

"He lifted me out of the ditch, pulled me from the deep mud.
He stood me up on a solid rock to make sure I wouldn't slip.
PSALM 40:2 THE MESSAGE

Ahhhhh...the HAPPY PLACE. Is it fictional? Is it real? Can we ever take up permanent residence there? Is it even a worthy goal for us as believers in Jesus Christ? I think these are great questions to address! In fact, let's start the discussion by asking ourselves some questions as we tackle FIVE THINGS that could be roadblocks in reaching that sought after destination.

1) YOU CHOOSE ONLY TO BE HAPPY ONCE EVERYTHING WORKS OUT.

Much of the time, our happiness is dependent upon what's happening around us. However, happiness that is birthed out of joy is determined by what's happening inside of you. Whatever our minds focus on, so there go our thoughts as well—which in turn affects our emotions. Are you focusing on what you don't have this very moment or being thankful for what you've been given as you wait for answered prayers?

2) YOU ARE STUCK IN YOUR PAST.

You can't start the next chapter of your life by continually re-reading your last one. Don't become a casualty of your past due to what if's, regret, sorrow and 20/20 hindsight. Let your past do the only job it's meant to do and that's to help you learn from it. Do you need to move on from anything?

3) YOU CHASE THE WRONG THINGS.

I read once that when you stop chasing the wrong things, you give the right things a chance to catch up with you. Taking an honest look at your goals, in a prayerful setting, can shed light on dreams and desires that may have you clinging to things that will never make you happy. Any 'idols' you need to toss out the window? Any plans for your life that don't have God's approval yet?

4) YOU HOLD GRUDGES.

As you may have heard before, holding a grudge equates to about the same logic as drinking poison and waiting for the other person to die. Let go of your bitterness toward that person or situation for your own benefit. Truth be told, they've probably moved on and could care less anyway. Doesn't that stink when you think about it?

5) YOU DON'T LEARN FROM YOUR MISTAKES.

You can't change what you refuse to confront. Maybe it's time to evaluate why the same things keep happening to you. Once you look honestly at any negative circumstances in your life, be willing to admit it if you are the common contributing denominator in these disappointments. Are you caught in a vicious cycle of continuing to make the same bad choices, yet still expecting a different result?

When you change your mindset, you change your course of direction. When you get honest with yourself and let the answers to these five questions 'shine some light' on where you currently reside, you may find you are all 'muddy' because of your own personal decisions. Let the GOLD that emerges from doing things God's way not only dig you out of a pit, but place your feet on the SOLID ROCK that provides you with unspeakable JOY instead of happiness. At the end of the day, happiness shouldn't be the destination we are seeking anyway. Undesired circumstances can rob that 'place of residence' every single time. But joy—that's the GOLD God gives in spite of our circumstances! It's tied to peace and contentment! Yep, that's where we all want to camp. And friend, when we get *there*, a rewarding BRIGHT AND BOLD HIGH 'FIVE' will definitely be in order!

Dear God, so many times I raise my fists to heaven and blame You because my life is a mess. However, I'm now seeing that examining my personal choices is a good first step to seeing lasting positive change in my life. Honoring You in every single decision I make is the only way to experience lasting peace and keep me on the right track. I give You permission to change any mindsets that don't honor You. Help me chase after the GOLD in your Word because that is where I will find the road map to true joy and lasting contentment. Amen

STORMY WEATHER

DAY 23

"But now thus says the Lord, He who created you..."Fear not,
for I have redeemed you; I have called you by name, you are
mine. When you pass through the waters, I will be with you; and
through the rivers, they shall not overwhelm you..."

ISAIAH 43:1-2A ESV

S ometimes when it rains, it pours. And because we know that the
chance of a storm is always possible, we need to be wise enough to
take advantage of the storm gear that's been provided to help us to ride
it out. And in order to make sure it's available to help us when we need
it, keeping that 'protection' within quick and easy reach at all times is
imperative.

The same principle is true in our everyday lives. We all understand
the reality that "storms in life" are going to come and go—manifesting
themselves as difficult circumstances, challenges and disappointments—
each of them with the ability to threaten our "opportunity to stay dry."
With that noted, there is a question that is begging to be asked. If you
were in a rainstorm and given an umbrella to get from point A to point
B, would you run through the storm, carrying it with you, but never

open it? Of course not! That would be the first thing you would do before you ever moved an inch forward! It would be your only chance of staying dry!

Let that same mindset carry over into the storms of life. We all have protective gear available to us. God's Word offers not only promises to stand on but instructions in the Bible on how to navigate these storms as well. Nevertheless, many of us run through our 'storms' and never open a Bible up—and then wonder why we are windblown and sopping wet as we wait for the stormy days to pass. It's interesting to note that several studies have found that almost 9 out of 10 households own a Bible and that the average household has three. However, the same studies also revealed that half of Americans have read little or none of the Bible. Many further admitted that even though they owned a Bible, their only interaction with scripture passages was through listening to a pastor's message—not opening a Bible for themselves.

You've heard it said. You are either coming out of a storm. You are in a storm. Or you are headed for a storm. Don't be caught unprotected. Keep your Bible close. And for goodness sake, open it up and READ IT! It will do you no good otherwise—just like a closed umbrella on a rainy day won't either. As you let this principle fall fresh on you today, remember this reality. In any storm, even with an umbrella, you are going to feel a few drops of rain. That is inevitable. But with the right equipment, not only do you come out with less 'storm damage', you're also dry and ready to go when the skies finally clear. And spending some valuable time in God's Word BEFORE THE STORM HITS, well, you never know, you might even find yourself 'singing in the rain'! (One worship song after another!!) That's the life changing GOLD perspective that knowing His promises can make!

If you are navigating some stormy weather right now, take heart. Brighter days are coming.

Lord, it's easy to run to just about everything but my Bible when challenging times hit. Drowning my anxious thoughts in tv shows, books and social media posts feel like relief at the time but they never fill my deep desire for peace in the midst of a stormy time in life. Only your promises can cover me and give me real hope I can hold on to. Though the other outlets aren't bad things, I pray they won't be my first lines of defense. As I place your scripture in my heart, I pray it will be like an umbrella that keeps me protected until I see those golden rays of sunshine again. Amen

DEEP END

DAY 24

"And we know that for those who love God all things work together for good, for those who are called according to His purpose. For those whom He foreknew He also predestined to be conformed to the image of His Son, in order that He might be the firstborn among many brothers. And those whom He predestined He also called, and those whom He called He also justified, and those whom He justified He also glorified."

ROMANS 8:28-30 ESV

G od doesn't just call the qualified. Sometimes he simply equips the called. And most times, it's a 'learn it by doing it' process. We have all heard the saying, "they just threw me into the deep end!" In those cases, one just has to learn as they go. But let's not forget. Anyone thrown into the deep end showed some promise somewhere along the way for anyone to want to 'toss them in' in the first place. So, what do you think? Called or Qualified? I think it is a little bit of both.

When you pause a moment to consider it, God actually takes the same approach when launching us into our destinies. We are going through life...many times in the 'school of hard knocks' hoping to be voted "Most

Likely to Survive"! And the next thing you know, 'opportunity knocks' instead. And sometimes it does more than knock. Maybe you, like me, have watched the door come right off the hinges! And rather than go, "hey, this is awesome!", we start trying to get it back up and nailed shut as quickly as possible so we don't have to ever worry about that darn thing ever opening back up again! Anybody else had that experience?

I formerly served as a Director of Women's Ministry at the north campus of a mega church in the Dallas area. I can tell you with confidence, that the position—by the world's standards—should have never been mine. Although I had been leading Bible studies for years, I had not been to Seminary—and I had no intention of adding a third degree to my resume! But as I prayerfully considered the position, God prompted me to write out a list of my life experiences that could affirm my ability to do the job. *That part* was easy to follow through on. But soon after completing it, the Holy Spirit prompted me to follow that list with the life experiences I felt might disqualify me. That, on the other hand, was zero fun. I bawled when I got through writing it. My first reaction was, "What in the world are you thinking, God? I have made way too many mistakes to have a position like that." However, by following through on that exercise, eventually God clearly revealed that my past heartbreaks and mishaps would actually be THE VERY THING that made me qualified to take on this ministry opportunity that now stood in front of me.

Why share all of this? My desire is to encourage you to fully trust God when He calls you to uncharted territories—not based on your talents and good stewardship—but sometimes specifically in spite of them. If God calls you to "the deep end of the pool", believe that He will give you what you need to do the task at hand. And just so you know, I am truly beginning to believe that He prefers to take us to places where we can't "swim" without His help! He knows full well that the more we have to depend on Him, the more we remember who gets the glory!

There's no doubt that He will call you to accomplish great things using your gifts and talents. But always remember that they're never the determining factor. Those attributes are merely methods to help communicate the redemptive, life-giving work He did for you, personally. It's the testimonies of that great work that will now go on to encourage the many people you will influence. They are the GOLD you now have to share.

We are positioned to be a lifeline for a lot of drowning people in our generation. So be brave and make your own life survey—fully aware that everything you list won't be "good". But do it believing that your God will absolutely work them together for your long-range benefit. God is the one who QUALIFIES. He even qualifies the qualified! Never forget that!

So, when He does call, because He will, put your GOLD dress on and jump in! You can even do a 'cannon ball' or a 'belly flop'! Just make sure you go ALL THE WAY IN! And once you have, give yourself the gift of 'floating' for a moment in His love for you. Focus on who He is—not who you are—because that is where true confidence is found. Oh, but I do have one request. When you do jump, will you please do it at the other end? This southern gal just got her hair done. And you know what they say? They higher the hair, the closer to God—and I know you wouldn't want to mess that up for me! Happy Swimming!

Father, I thank you that you truly do use all things and work them together for good so that many can see your redemptive work on display. Help me to base my worth in that work and not determine my value through the lens of my mistakes. I thank you for the GOLD treasure—laced with empathy and wisdom— that I have gained through every good and bad experience in my life. Use each of them to draw others closer to You. I'm ALL IN on YOUR PLAN. Amen

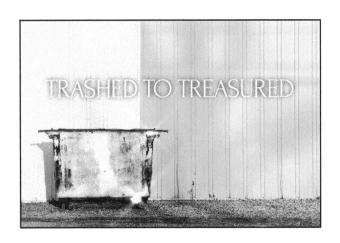

DAY 25

*"Forget about what's happened; don't keep going over old history.
Be alert, be present. I'm about to do something brand-new. It's
bursting out! Don't you see it? There it is! I'm making
a road through the desert, rivers in the badlands."*

ISAIAH 43:19 THE MESSAGE

M y precious, wonderful and amazing husband started doing a careless, annoying and frustrating thing—he kept taking his wedding
ring off and playing with it. This seemingly "no big deal" act eventually
resulted in his ring getting laid around in places it wasn't supposed to be.
Cue the statement you already knew was coming: "Baby, have you seen
my wedding ring?" To which my response was probably much like yours
would have been: "Well, you shouldn't have been so careless with it when
you took it off." Sigh. And then the hunt began. I helped him look for a
while—but then he started a relentless hunt of his own. He looked for
hours. Then woke up in the night so baffled and frustrated, that he got
up and started looking for it again. That next morning over coffee, he
regretfully shared with me how devastated he was that he couldn't find
his ring. I knew he was, so I tried hard not to add to his misery with
my own statements of how sick I was about this loss as well. Soon after

our conversation, I left for my morning walk, where during my trek, I asked the Lord repeatedly (as if He is hard of hearing) to help us find the wedding ring. I also confessed, *repeatedly*, that I knew He was perfectly aware of where the ring was and asked Him to reveal it to Gary. There was no doubt in my mind that the situation had been covered *adequately* in prayer. I had a trail of sweat following five miles behind me to prove it.

I'll never forget the scene of when I came home from my walk. My clothes were drenched and I was heading straight for the shower. I had to pass Gary's office where a chair that I hated "lived". When I say I despised this chair, I mean that I vowed it would be the first thing to go when a few of our "big prayers" were answered regarding our future. The faux leather was peeling off, leaving a full visual of the foam behind it. It was pitiful looking at best. The very sight of it struck utter disbelief that it was even in my house. It was a daily reminder that our prayers had not yet been answered because Gary had 'chosen not to replace it' until our current situation was resolved. I remember walking past that chair and thinking, "Ugh...I hate that chair." And then I kept going toward our bedroom and jumped in the shower to get ready for the day.

Later that morning, when I was doing my quiet time, guess who came running into the room with his wedding ring on his finger? Yep, God had answered our prayers! But how and where he found "the answer" was the more incredible part of the story. It ends up that the ring had fallen on to the floor in his office and got hung-up between one of the caster wheels on that ugly worn out office chair. (Yes, the one I would have thrown in the dumpster that morning if I would have been given 'the green light'.) Gary had rolled that chair around a million times looking for the ring on that floor. But while working at the computer, he felt The Lord say, "turn the chair upside down". In his mind, he brushed it off at first because he had already looked in the cushions and didn't find the ring. But the feeling wouldn't go away. So, he finally got up and turned it over thinking he was waiting for it to fall out of the chair cushions. As he glanced around the edge of the chair to look for the ring on the floor, something shiny caught his eye. There sat that ring imbedded in the caster wheel of the chair. It was an unbelievable find—totally undetectable except that the Lord told him to look there. To say we were both elated would be an understatement! However, God was teaching us so much more through that experience. Things much deeper than just an answer to our prayers. In fact, they may be some great lessons for you too.

First, when we are careless with precious things, they can be lost. Anything precious in your life that you have been careless with? Be careful to cherish and protect those people and things you love so that you don't find them "lost forever" one day.

Second, sometimes what we are looking for is right where we are. We have to be patient and wait for God to reveal it.

Third, be careful not to despise the provisions God has currently given you. The answers to your prayers could be attached to them or concealed in them. Is there anything or anyone in your life that you despise and are ready to throw away? Be careful here. They just might hold the answer to your prayers. Choose to be grateful and thankful in ALL THINGS so you don't eliminate His ability to bless you through them.

Fourth, when God says to do something, no matter how ridiculous it may seem and no matter how many times you feel like you have already done it, just do it anyway. Revelations from Him are always preceded by our obedience to first do what He asks us to do. Is God telling you to "try" one more time, but you are ready to throw in the towel? If He says, "don't give up" or "go back again", just do it. Don't let your pride or human reasoning get in the way of your obedience. If God prompts you to do something, it's always a request marked with purpose and greater good on the other side of your follow through.

In regards to my Gary, I don't think I've ever witnessed more relief on his face than I did the morning he found that ring. The revelation for me personally? I started looking at that chair differently than I did before this happened. I finally realized that one day, when the timing was right, it would go to that 'great dumpster in the sky'! (And when it eventually did, I won't lie. I did not shed a tear.) But until that glorious moment arrived, my perspective of that shabby chair was forever changed moving forward.

Instead, I saw it as a reminder- every day- of an answered prayer—not an unanswered one. However, I'm still in awe of the most precious lesson God wanted me to come away with: what we need is not hidden from God, though it may be hidden from us at the moment. My understanding of that truth is helping me to be more watchful for the sometimes 'unconventional ways' He may decide to reveal His answers. And to think—*if I would've had my way*—that chair would have been thrown away that morning—along with the answer to our prayers! Crazy to even fathom!

God was doing something new in the midst of something old. He was making a way where there seemed to be no way. He was bringing forth "OUR GOLD TREASURE", Gary's wedding band, through something I was ready to TRASH! And friend, be assured, God is making a way for you too—very possibly in the most unlikely places.

Heavenly Father, 24k lessons are waiting for me if I allow myself to be Your student. Thank you that You are bringing forth GOLD in my circumstances—even when all hope seems to be lost. I'm in awe that you absolutely answer prayer. It thrills my soul to realize that there is nothing that You can't use to accomplish Your purposes. Thank you for taking my trash and turning it into treasure on a daily basis. You are my Lord, my Rock and my Redeemer. Amen

LESS BITTER
MORE GLITTER

DAY 26

"A person's insight gives him patience, and his
virtue is to overlook an offense."

PROVERBS 19:11 HCSB

I don't know about you, but I'm literally exhausted from seeing the hate and discord that exists between people in our world. I know it must grieve God because His Word has SO MUCH to say about it! Overlooking an offense is one of the most UNNATURAL things you will ever discipline yourself to do. But let's be challenged today with a new perspective on difficult individuals and the challenges that can stem from our interactions with them.

Let's start by thinking of someone whose ideas or actions are offensive to you. Maybe even someone who may have actually hurt or disappointed you personally with their words or inconsiderate choices. Now ask yourself this question: If I spent half as much time praying for this person as I do complaining about them, how much further along might they be? If nothing else, how much further along MIGHT I BE by climbing out of this pit of misery I've made myself at home in?

Here's one more question for you while we're at it. Have you ever taken the time to think about why this trend of bitterness in today's culture never ends? The reality lies in the fact that many of us are caught in a vicious cycle of bitterness because no one will go first and let the offense go. The need to be right. The need to have the last word. The need to be heard. They've all become greater than the need to find a resolution.

So, what do you say? Let's give God's way of "handling hurt" a try. Any time we feel the urge to take offense, let it be a trigger to pray instead. Every time you are ready to go through the roof over commentary on the news, turn it off and walk away. Choose not to participate in negative banter on Social Media. Just don't even read it if you can't refrain from commenting. Practice holding your tongue when a face-to-face conversation gets heated. Be wise rather than undisciplined. Be guarded rather than defensive. The enemy of our soul knows he can negatively dominate our relationships and our overall outlook on the future if he can keep us in discord. Our friends and family need a glimpse of this GOLD we have to offer. In fact, the whole world needs it.

Starting today...let's choose LESS BITTER and MORE GLITTER. Follow Christ's lead on this subject and make room for His principles to have a positive effect on others. In the process, you'll also free yourself from the bondage of your own negative reactions. And when this attitude becomes a way of life, get ready for the "fall out" that your personal obedience brings. The outcome will be a 'sparkly mess' you won't mind leaving behind.

Dear Father, bitterness is such a vicious emotion—and I don't want it to take root in my heart. Anytime I feel the need to hold on to resentment toward someone, I ask that you will help me remember to turn it into an opportunity to pray for them instead. I ask that You disarm the enemy before he has a chance to damage my relationships and tarnish my testimony in order that I can be a shining reflection of You. Rather than throwing harsh words out at others in frustration, give me the grace to throw a "glitter bomb" instead. Help me look for resolutions instead of paybacks. Bring forth GOLD in me that can only come from spending time with you. Amen

ALL THAT GLITTERS

DAY 27

"You say, "I am allowed to do anything"-but not everything
is good for you. You say, "I am allowed to do anything"
-but not everything is beneficial."

1 COR 10:23 NMB

O k, can I be the first to say...WHYYYYYYYY? Why can't these sparkly, sweet and delicious delectables be good for you??? Although I can't answer the "why", I can attest to the fact that they are NOT going to be your friends after consumption—no matter what your eyes might be telling you!

The enemy has been working to convince us for a long time—actually since the Garden of Eden—that the things we think we WANT are actually what we NEED in order to be satisfied. He whispers in our ears that we deserve the things we earnestly desire and that we won't be happy unless we have them. His intent is to tempt us to compromise our resolve with things that will be to our personal detriment. And it satisfies him even more if our actions end up negatively affecting others as well.

For some of you, it's not a donut. Instead, it's a drink. For others it's that new car. Maybe it's a bigger house. For another, it's that designer bag. Each of these things potentially has the power to put you in bondage to something—whether it is a treadmill, an AA meeting or the credit card company of your choice. But this is where things get tricky. What puts me in bondage may be no biggie for you and vice versa. It would be great if there was an official and complete list of everything you can and can't have in order to live a happy and bondage-free life. The problem is, we're all different. Each of us lives with individual body makeups, chemical balances and monthly incomes. It could even be that some of you are in transition periods that beg for temporary boundaries where there could have been 'yeses' just a few months ago. Some of us work within the bounds of another's expectations. Many of us battle with temptation as we try to reach a personal goal while others resist the enjoyment of doing something on behalf of the many people who see them as a role model. But there is one thing we most likely have in common: There is always something we feel like we want but we can't have.

In a world full of grey areas and sparkly things that beg for our attention, I urge you to ask God what He thinks about any decision you make. That may sound tedious but hear me out. Remember that just because you can, doesn't mean you should. Just because someone else is 'doing it' or 'gets to have it' does not mean it's the best thing for you. Maybe its timing. Maybe it's going to bring more harm to you and others than you realize. Maybe it will cause someone else to fall into bondage. But we can be sure of this: we are always weighing out poor, good or BEST decisions. So, train yourself to ask these three questions:

1) Does this confirm what God told me to do?
2) Would someone further along than me agree with my decision?
3) Does it hinder my opportunity to glorify God?

When we pause to ask God what He thinks in our everyday decisions, He always guides us to the BEST CHOICE. The life-giving choice. The choice that sets us up to be a blessing to others. And as for the gorgeous donuts in this photo, don't give in and eat them. They will show up again later—in places where they weren't invited. Never forget: ALL THAT GLITTERS IS NOT GOLD.

Lord, we hear the saying "the heart wants what the heart wants" thrown around all the time as an excuse to do what we want to do. But I want my heart to want what Your heart wants—which is what will be beneficial for me in the long run. Purify my motives and my reasoning skills until they become catalysts for seeing things from your perspective. Help me to accept a "no" when it comes from You so I can stay hindrance-free and ready for any GOLDEN OPPORTUNITIES You send my way! Amen

GOLD DIGGER

DAY 28

"Cling to wisdom—she will protect you. Love her—she will guard
you. Getting wisdom is the most important thing
you can do! And with your wisdom, develop
common sense and good judgment."

PROVERBS 4:6-7 TLB

D id you know that wisdom is calling your name? She may look a little different than the perspective the world gives—and this timeless wisdom may not always be found on Pinterest or in the latest and greatest selling self-help book. However, this shiny treasure is most definitely found throughout the pages of Proverbs in the Old Testament. This amazing book of the Bible has the ability to pierce our hearts with moral insight and purposeful guidelines for living. And the coolest thing: because there are thirty-one chapters, there is one for each day of the month!

There is so much knowledge packed within these chapters of Proverbs that you could read it throughout your lifetime and never exhaust the treasures they provide. It was written by three authors: Agur, King Lemuel, and primarily by King Solomon...who is known to be the wisest man who ever lived! How 'bout that? The pages are filled with promises, warnings, skills and practices for living wisely. These impartations are targeted at the hearts and minds of both men and women—all with the goal of help-ing us become more like Christ. Would you like to have the tools to live life from a healthier, smarter, and wiser perspective? I thought you might! Here are just a few ways that I continue to gain deeper understanding of Godly wisdom and NEVER GET BORED WITH IT EITHER!

1) One of my favorite things to do is to pick a word to watch for throughout each chapter that month. For instance, one month, I marked the word "heart" with a pink highlighter when I found it in a verse. Before I knew it, I could—and actually still can—look back and see a pattern of what love looks like in the context of Godly wisdom. You might notice a word like "knowledge" or maybe even "beware" and that can be your "gold nugget" to search for that month. The goal is to keep your eyes from glazing over the passages because you have read them before.

2) Try reading a different translation of the Bible each month. One month, I might read it from the NIV. The next month it might be from The Message. The subtle changes in presentation of God's Word can open up brand new insights!

3) Try taking a month and listening to a chapter each day through a Bible app on your phone or computer. It can be soothing and peaceful to close your eyes and just listen to God's precious words as if He were talking to you Himself. You can also listen on your way to a meeting or in the carpool line while you wait for your kids! It's a great way to change it up!

4) Choose a month to write down guidelines that stand out to you personally as you read each day. If you keep a special journal for your study of Proverbs, over time you can look back and see the lessons God is teaching you. I like to date mine as well so I can see my progress in specific areas and reminders of things I still need to work on. It can turn into your personal handbook for Godly living.

5) Look for a Bible Study that specifically concentrates on the book

of Proverbs. Examining this special book from another's fresh perspective can enhance your overall understanding as well!

6) One month, get a 'Proverbs Group' together where you read the scriptures on your own time. At some point in the day, text the group your stand-out verse for that day. It's a great way to have accountability and to encourage each other along the way.

7) Focusing on learning different concepts within each chapter can also enhance your overall understanding of wisdom. Take a month to focus on 'instructions'. Maybe focus on 'consequences' the next month. On one round of study, you could write down everything you learn about God that month. You can record these things in the margins of your Bible or in a special journal or notebook. You not only have something to go back and read later but it also helps you to better remember the lessons when you write them down.

No matter what method you choose, it's the "digging" that counts. That's how you find the GOLD treasure of Godly wisdom! In fact, why not start today and begin with the chapter that corresponds with today's date! This is a VERY DOABLE PRACTICE that enables the wisdom of God's Word to become second nature in your heart. If you commit to a year of this treasure hunting, you'll be thrilled at the results! And while you're on this fabulous quest for wisdom, take some extra care in that 31st chapter. If we can get the model of a Godly woman ingrained in our day-to-day life, there's no telling what The Lord might be able to accomplish through us!! Happy hunting to all of you GOLD DIGGERS! Treasure upon treasures await you in the months to come!

Lord, You tell me that wisdom is supreme—and I want to learn at the highest level so I can do everything with excellence. I pray that You will guard me from the complacency and pride that would convince me that I know enough to get by on my own. Give me a passion to dig for the GOLD treasure that can only be found in Your Word. My goal is to be a millionaire in You. Amen

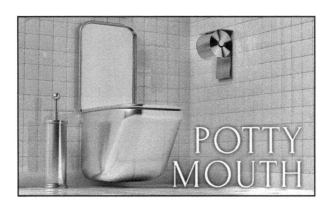

POTTY MOUTH

DAY 29

"Do not let any unwholesome talk come out of your mouths, but only what is helpful for building others up according to their needs, that it may benefit those who listen."

EPHESIANS 4:29 NIV

Ahhhhhh, the infamous potty mouth. We've all probably laughed at the funny quote that says, "I love Jesus but I cuss a little." AND YES, my sweet momma had to call me out on that as a teenage girl when I let a 'not so ladylike word' fall from my lips in her presence. Have you ever said something and wished you could have inhaled it back in just as quickly and easily as it fell off your lips? I can STILL see the look on her face and I can STILL see her mouth moving in response: "Young lady, if you talk like that around your friends, it's going to slip out with ease around others too." I'm actually shaking again just typing this! But all joking aside. Isn't it something how those teachable moments—though they 'stink'—seem to be the most impactful?

You know, I learned a huge practical lesson in that moment. But, I've also found that God would like to bring a little more to the conversation regarding our potty mouths. Because, in reality, a potty mouth tells on itself with more than just profanity. In fact, it actually takes on many forms much more destructive than a curse word here and there. For many, using foul language has never been an issue. Instead, that offensive 'potty odor' is manifesting itself in less obvious ways. It may look more like gossip. Or maybe like slander. Maybe it's angry words or back-stabbing. Maybe a potty mouth is showing up in racist remarks or statements made out of our own insecurity that end up betraying and hurting others.

So, let's not be fooled by the so-called subtlety of our words. They have destroyed many friendships along with countless reputations. Through careless "dirty" words, trust has been broken and bitterness has been given root in our marriages, with our kids, in our churches and in our workplaces. When we neglect our relationship with Christ on the inside, it shows on the outside. When we don't let him refine every detail of our being, that 'potty of a mouth' just might OVERFLOW—and we all know that's not only messy, but stinky and a pain in the proverbial "behind" to clean up!

So, let's give ourselves an easy standard to live by: If it won't honor God, let's FLUSH IT! If it's not constructive and edifying, down the drain it goes—gone forever. Let's allow the ultimate 'Mr. Clean' to do some much needed sanitizing in our hearts and minds. Let's make sure our mouths leave no 'scum' in sight—only a shiny GOLD reflection of God's Word coming alive in us. That mindset will result in a sparkling clean 'aroma' that everyone will welcome.

Lord, I ask for forgiveness for the many times my speech has left a stench in the room. Help me to sense when my frustrations and bad attitudes are turning my mouth into a 'potty'. I give you permission to scrub my mouth so clean that it's unrecognizable to those who know me best. Because if it measures up to your standards with them, I know I'm ready to be influential with others. Amen

DAY 30

"Now faith is the assurance of things hoped for,
the conviction of things not seen."

HEB 11:1 ESV

Has The Lord ever called you to consider stepping out in an area that feels way out of your comfort zone? Oh gosh! I know I have! I get filled with excitement at the initial thought! I've been known to jump up and down with joy before I quickly sit down to start researching and brainstorming all of the inspired details. That creative process is absolutely exhilarating to me! Are you like that too? But friend, for me personally, that high tends to nose-dive and crash the minute I start to think about how this mega idea will need to be accomplished. As frustrating as that can be, you can't ignore the elephant in the room—and that's the huge gap between getting an idea and actually seeing that idea come to fruition. And whether you are scared or exhilarated after God gives you a divine directive, there is one inevitable piece of the process that must take place before you see any results. At some point, you have to START.

Taking the first step in any venture is the hardest part of being obedient. If you are anything like me, you're constantly weighing the pros and cons of every idea—so stepping out feels paralyzing. There's always an excuse not to move forward, right? In fact, you may even see yourself in one or more of the following statements:

Afraid of making the wrong choice, so you fail to make one at all.
Petrified of failure, so you don't try.
Anxious over the unknown, so you stick with what you do know.
Worried others will think it's a dumb idea, so you decide it's probably a dumb idea.
You can't be sure of a fairytale ending, so you just close the book.

The root of SOME of these excuses is that little "P" word that brings about anything but 'little' consequences—and that's Pride. But you know what I've also learned? EVERY step of faith not taken is ALWAYS rooted in a big "F" word...and that's FEAR. That's the enemy's playground! And although he begs you to come and play with him, we can all be certain of this—He will never let you win at anything while you're there.

But do you know what I want us to realize? Recess on that playground is over. Didn't you hear it? The bell rang and it's time to go back to class and learn what God's Word has to say about FAITH!! That's the "F" word God wants you reciting instead of fear. Truth is, everything is hard before it's easy. Think about that for a minute. No one starts at anything as an expert. Many have failed more times than not before they experienced success in a venture. But this is the bottom line: Everything that God calls you to do takes a first step. None of us hit our stride sitting on the sidelines. No one experiences a breakthrough without a follow through. Nobody gets to the other side without moving forward. Not a single person advances without stepping out. No one has a story worth telling if they've failed to take the adventure.

"You don't have to see the whole staircase to take the first step."
-Martin Luther King, Jr.

So today, ask the Lord to light your path. Then put your favorite pair of GOLD shoes on and take a step of faith—remembering that YOUR GOD (and mine!) is bigger than any honest mistake you could ever make. Do it in heels or do it in tennis shoes. But someone reading this today needs to 'JUST DO IT'! Go get'em, girl!

Heavenly Father, if YOU call me to it, YOU will bring me through it. Thank you that I can depend on that. I pray right now that fear and procrastination will not be my narrative. I ask that my faith in YOU will be strengthened in the process. You promise to light my path—one step at a time. Help me to focus on doing the things of the moment with excellence, knowing that those very practices are building my character and preparing me for the next step of faith. Amen

GET YOUR HANDS DIRTY

DAY 31

"Then they will answer him, 'When, Lord, did we ever see you
hungry or thirsty or a stranger or naked or sick or in
prison, and we would not help you?' The King will reply,
'I tell you, whenever you refused to help one of these
least important ones, you refused to help me.'

MATTHEW 25:44-45 GNT

Throughout our lives, we have all been instructed on the importance of cleanliness. If you are breathing you have been taught that 'being' clean or 'getting' clean is a top priority AND the ultimate goal we're trying to reach. Both 'CLEAN your room' or 'CLEAN your plate' were probably stressed more than once growing up. And I'm sure you've been asked the following questions as well. Did you CLEAN behind your ears? Did you CLEAN the car? I can remember my dad asking me to do everything from 'CLEAN the pool' to 'CLEAN up my act!'. Then moving into adulthood, the word clean started getting used in other ways. Like, 'did you get a CLEAN bill of health?' Or 'we are going to start with a CLEAN slate.' Furthermore, we have also been relieved to learn through God's Word that we can be washed completely CLEAN of the sins of our past and have a thriving relationship with the God of the universe if we accept Jesus as our personal Savior. Let's face it, CLEAN is valuable!!

But today, we are going to throw caution to the wind and forget about the priority of being clean. In fact, I want to encourage you to "wash that word" right out of your mind. Instead of keeping our hands 'clean and sanitized', let's GET OUR HANDS DIRTY! Let's leave a reflection of Jesus in impactful ways without even having to say His name.

Getting your hands dirty could be spending time with someone that lives alone. It might be teaching a young woman a few steps behind you how to study her Bible like you do. It could mean delivering dinners. Maybe it's inviting and attending an event with a woman that would never go if you didn't invest your time and money into her personal growth. You might be prompted to clean someone's house after their surgery or the birth of a child. It could mean to stop what you are focused on long enough to make that phone call or send that text of inquiry when the Lord brings someone to your mind. It could be to finally make a financial investment into your local church rather than staying a full-time consumer of the resources they are offering. Only you will know how the Lord is prompting you to show His love. But be willing to make room for the opportunities that come your way. In fact, I would encourage you to do more than just make room for them. Ask for them! For some of us who are 'professing' Christians, it's probably high time we put some skin in the game when it comes to being the hands and feet of Jesus.

"Remember that you never look into the eyes of someone God does not love."

-TruthToTable

So actually look into those eyes. Allow God to work through you in tangible ways. PRAYER IS POWERFUL! In fact, God's Word tells us it moves mountains! But so do our HANDS for people who need to see Jesus in tangible ways. What do I mean by that? For a single mom, your prayers are a vital part of her encouragement and support. But if you were sensitive to the immediate need in her life, offering to babysit her children while she goes out to dinner with a friend or enjoys a cup of coffee in the solitude of her EMPTY AND QUIET car would probably make her feel seen and loved by Jesus more than anything. That's just one example, but I think you get the gist of what I'm saying.

Yep, there are times that investing in others is going to get messy... maybe messy like a poopy diaper! But don't get labeled as being "all talk and no action." Don't be tempted to think that communication with the Lord on their behalf is all God might be calling you to do. Be willing to recognize when you have your hands clasped tightly "in the name of prayer" in order to keep them from "getting dirty" in the NAME OF LOVE. There is no better day than today to give away the GOLD.

Heavenly Father, I throw the word 'love' around way to easily at times. I pray that my actions will live up to my speech—and that my actual deeds will match my level of empathy. It's easy to assume that someone else can take care of all the needs we see around us every day. Allow me to love others with more than just a sentiment in my heart. I want action to be witnessed by others who need your love instead of just living out my days being proud of my good intentions. Help me 'give away the gold' in tangible ways when it's within my power to do it. Amen

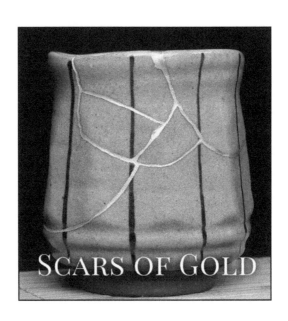

SCARS OF GOLD

DAY 32

"Come and listen, all you who fear God,
and I will tell you what He did for me."

PSALM 66:16 NLT

I had the privilege of doing an "adult sleepover" with about twenty women a few weeks ago. A new friend in ministry invited us—all speakers and worship leaders—into her home with the sole intent of providing mutual encouragement and a place to find community with other gals who have the same calling. It was a beautiful weekend of testimonies and worship—and as you can imagine—lots of words! Everyone was sharing pieces of their stories along with the projects and ministries they were devoted to. I watched God's Word come alive that weekend as I observed that iron truly does sharpen iron as we've learned in Proverbs 27:17. After sharing my vision and heart behind the book you are now reading, God used a new friend to introduce me to an artform that blew me away.

Kintsugi is the traditional Japanese art of repairing broken ceramics using, of all things, GOLD! This ancient practice, dating back to the 15th Century, applies a precious metal – liquid gold, liquid silver or lacquer dusted with powdered gold—to not only mend the piece of pottery but to also enhance the places where the pottery was broken. This beautiful and unique technique not only repairs the original piece, it also gives it a new and more refined look. In fact, the random and irregular way each piece shatters is what makes it a stunning one-of-a-kind piece of art. The genius behind the artform is to *expose* the flaws, not hide them and pretend they aren't there. The artisan intentionally highlights them with a gold bond that not only catches your eye, it actually draws your attention to the individuality and beauty that was born from these unintended breaks. The result is nothing short of stunning.

What can you and I learn about our lives and God's handiwork from these Kintsugi artists? We spend so much of our lives as women looking for ways to hide the areas where we have been broken. We work to stuff, burn, bury, demolish and extinguish any record of our past to make sure we look "perfect" to those who see us. We focus on the fact that we are a "new creature in Christ", so we will never need to remember or speak of those broken places again. We do all of this believing that is what will make us worthy of respect—or at least a second chance in life. But in the back of our minds, no matter what we do, we seem to never be able to forget who we used to be. Behind the scenes, it cripples us and we feel frustrated. It can even causes a tension between us and God. We begin to question Him: Why can't I move on from this?? You said that you cast my sin as far as the east is from the west. If so, then why can't I forget it? Why does this still feel attached to me? If you have ever struggled in this area, I truly understand. God, in the merciful way that He does, has been shedding some light on this subject for me. I hope it will encourage you as well.

God is self-sustaining. He CAN forget when He chooses. He IS God— He can do anything. That is the promise—that He will remember your sin no more. What a gift! However, we as humans are not God. We were not made to forget. On the contrary, we were MADE TO REMEMBER. Let's begin unpacking this from a practical standpoint. We would grab hot curling irons over and over again if we could forget they will blister our hands when we touch them. Point being, God gave us a memory to keep us from making painful mistakes again and again. Secondly, we were made to remember so we as humans won't forget what God has done for us. It helps us keep a crystal clear perspective—which leads to a greater reverence for the miracles He has performed in us. In fact, our memory can be the sole agent that protects us from becoming prideful and thinking we are little "mini me" gods. But the greatest reason to remember is that those "scars of gold" are meant to tell a story to others. They are meant to be used for a greater glory than our own. They are the catalyst that draws another in so they can see the art that God makes with broken things. If we forget where we've been and what He's brought us through, then there is no story to tell.

God not only wants to mend your broken pieces, He wants to highlight them with GOLD. He wants people to SEE His handiwork and the beauty that has come from His intervention. It's time many of us remember, that before Him, we were a broken vessel. And now, because of Him, we're not only intact, we are a stunning piece of art.

So instead of trying to hide the fact that you were once broken, share what God has taught you about His heart, His forgiveness and His grace through mending your brokenness. Don't hold back your story—WHEN HE PROMPTS YOU TO SHARE—especially when you know it has the power to set another woman free. That testimony is laced with SOLID GOLD grace that makes you an original work of art. Let's be bold like that kind of gold. Because, just as the ancient Japanese Kintsugi artists knew: the *result* of their work is stunning. However, the *purpose* of their work was to *see the art put on display for others to view and appreciate.* Any other result contradicts the passion behind creating the art in the first place.

The work God has done in YOU is a priceless gift to those in your area of influence. Those gold scars tell a story. They make your contribution to

God's kingdom purposes unique. Don't tuck your story away on a shelf. Don't get amnesia in regards to all of the things God has transformed in your life. Allow them to be GOLD ON DISPLAY so that others can appreciate and marvel at the handiwork of our mighty God.

Lord, thank you for my scars of gold. Without them, I would have no proof of your love and compassion for me. Give me the courage to share my past with others instead of pretending it didn't happen—especially when another is facing adversity. The GOLD You have given me is surely a treasure worth displaying. Help me to live in awe of Your handiwork instead of looking for ways to hide my past in order to appear unscathed in the eyes of others. Amen

FOLLOW ME

DAY 33

"You're going to find that there will be times when people will have no stomach for solid teaching, but will fill up on spiritual junk food—catchy opinions that tickle their fancy. They'll turn their backs on truth and chase mirages."

2 TIMOTHY 4:3-4 THE MESSAGE

Today, we live and die by "LIKES". We accept, reject or show our indifference everyday with the click of a button, or lack thereof. And all of those 'heart eyes', 'thumbs up', 'faces that laugh until they cry', 'sad faces' and 'oh my gosh' emojis—well, they ultimately revolve around who we are FOLLOWING.

You all know the gig. If you have a relationship from the past or meet someone new, chances are in this day and time, you will go online and FOLLOW them on any one or all of the social media venues. Once you officially go in and 'follow' them, you regularly see the information they are sharing. That relationship of 'following' and 'liking' continues, much of the time, for years. And as those years move forward, usually only one thing can change that long-time camaraderie and friendship. And we all know what that is, right? YOU STOP LIKING WHAT YOU ARE

SEEING. And then what happens? The 'likes' from you become fewer. Maybe you put them on 'snooze'. You might even 'hide their posts for 30 days'. And if you are really frustrated by what you see, you can do the ultimate: UNFOLLOW THEM!

In a world where people and things can be instantly removed from our line of sight because WE DECIDE it's not worthy of our "likes" anymore, let's be careful not to apply that same rule of thumb to our relationship with the Lord. When we first accept Christ, we are convinced we will always FOLLOW HIM forever! Then, all of the sudden, He says, "Hey, I want you to give up __." or "I need you to forgive __." Next thing you know, we're like, "Ummm, HECK NO!"—and we click "UNFOLLOW" real quick and walk away. But please, don't be tempted to put a snooze on your time with Him. Don't hide for 30 days when His Word challenges what you "LIKE". And whatever you do, don't be tempted to completely walk away from any exposure to His loving guidance by 'UNFOLLOWING' Him. Instead, let's choose to FOLLOW HIM ALL THE DAYS OF OUR LIVES!! And maybe as those days pass, our beaten paths—following close after Him—will leave a visible trail of GOLD behind that encourages others to FOLLOW HIM too.

Father, thank you for allowing me the privilege of following You. I ask that anytime I get side-tracked, I will be quick to hear your redirection. I pray that my level of obedience will rise to meet your love for me. May I live in such a way that others want to follow You too. Amen

BE DIFFERENT

DAY 34

"That you may be blameless and innocent, children of God with-
out blemish in the midst of a crooked and twisted
generation, among whom you shine as lights in the world..."

PHILIPPIANS 2:15 ESV

Have you ever had the lyrics of a song seem to be on repeat? Playing over and over again in your brain as if it were taking up permanent residence. Several years ago, a popular Christian music artist released a song that I couldn't get out of my head. It spoke of being changed. Becoming different. It challenged us to let God remove anything in us that resembles "us" instead of Him. To be such a bright light in the world that everyone could see the difference He has made in us. Those lyrics not only became an anthem to my heart—they also began to challenge my whole view on how I interact with others. I'm wondering if our discussion today will resonate with you as well.

Different. It's a word that is getting a lot of discussion across social media platforms and in the press—tending to light a controversial fire any time it's tackled—challenging people to immediately take sides and draw lines in the sand. But as individuals who desire to be marked as

Christ followers, may I challenge you with a new perspective on the word "different"? In fact, instead of tackling what it does mean, what if we take a look at what it shouldn't mean to those of us who desire to represent Jesus well?

As Christians, 'different' from others shouldn't mean 'acting perfect', or 'religious', or 'holier than thou'. It shouldn't mean being in 'public judgement' of others. Nor should it require us to walk around, waving a bible in our hands, using harsh tones as we inform every one of the fiery fate that awaits them if they don't get it together! Instead, what if it meant shining a light onto the miracle God is performing in us? I like to think of it being a lot like the reward system I put in place for my students when I was teaching 2nd Grade. The benefits and perks came to them if I "caught them being good".

Let's imagine we stood out as "different" by allowing others to 'catch us' being transformed by the power of His Word—because it's become the foundation of our choices. Maybe they observe us trusting God with the 'un-trustables' rather than wringing our hands like everyone would expect—all because His Word says 'be anxious for nothing'. It would be refreshing if they caught us choosing to extend grace to people—who by all practical measures don't deserve it—because His Word says 'that by loving them you inturn love me'. It could simply be our own friends and family seeing us look past our pain as we honestly acknowledge that all things are not good, but still being full of joy because His Word says that 'if we are His, ALL things will be worked together for our good'.

It's so important to grasp that "different" does not automatically mean 'separation from others'. It's 'faith in the midst of others' in our everyday lives that sets a believer in Christ apart. God does the work. We just reflect Him. We are all sinners. Believers in Christ just happen to be aware of His saving grace and take full advantage of that gift. So, what do you say? Let's stand out like that. And out of all the black eggs people may come across in this lifetime, let's be the GOLD one.

Father, how lucky are we to have been fortunate enough to experience the saving grace You offer to anyone who desires to acknowledge You as their Savior. Help me to remember that setting myself apart and creating Christian social clubs was never a part of your plan to save the world. Remind me daily that living out my faith—not standing as everyone else's judge and jury—is the most effective way to share your love. Help me reflect YOUR GOLD in a world that needs You as desperately as I did the day my life was forever changed. I pray I'm caught today being humble, kind and full of the same grace You've shown me. Amen

COST ANALYSIS

DAY 35

*"For I am not ashamed of the gospel, because it is the power of
God that brings salvation to everyone who believes."*

ROMANS 1:16 NIV

What is your excuse for not being more proactive about sharing your faith in Jesus Christ? I realize, it's a bold question to start our time together today. However, it's a question begging to be answered if we are going to live a 24k life.

I've personally heard most of the excuses—and probably said them all in my mind a few times too. In fact, you could probably name some along with me. They come in many forms ranging from "I don't know enough scriptures to lead someone to Christ" to "I don't want to make people uncomfortable" to "isn't that the preacher's job to save people?". If you've had the "everyone else can take care of that" syndrome, unfortunately, you are not alone in the least. However, the excerpt that follows should be a 'wrecking ball' to the tidy little Christian excuses we give. When I read it, it sure put a crack in my glass jar of cop outs.

"If you believe there's a heaven and a hell, and people could be going to hell or not getting eternal life, and you think that it's not really

*worth telling them this because it would make it socially awkward...
how much do you have to hate somebody to believe everlasting life
is possible and not tell them that? I mean, if I believed, beyond the
shadow of a doubt, that a truck was coming at you, and you didn't
believe the truck was bearing down on you, there's a certain point
where I tackle you. And this is more important than that."*

Outspoken magician and atheist, Penn Jillette

How much do you have to HATE somebody to believe everlasting life
is possible and not tell them about it? Are you kidding me? You may be
having the same thoughts I did: I don't "hate anybody that bad"—or do
I? Or, do I just care that little about other people? Yeah, you're getting it.
There is no acceptable answer for our lack of urgency, is there?

God positions people in our lives—along with the opportunities to
intentionally share Jesus with them. They are friends, co-workers, family
members, neighbors and the like. And yet, we don't ever bring 'the subject' up. We look for every way to avoid it so they don't think we are being
weird or pushy or offensive. We don't mind bringing up that we go to
church...but we try not to get much deeper than that "for their sakes". We
wouldn't want to make them not "like us" anymore. Right? But truthfully,
I think we have to ask ourselves a question? Who is it that we are really
trying to 'save'? Because it surely isn't them. Ninety-nine percent of the
time, if we were honest, "saving face" for ourselves is more important than
sharing God's "saving grace" with others. It's sad—but true.

My challenge today is quite simple. When God provides the moment
to share your relationship with Jesus, don't shy away from it. Don't be
deceived into believing that it's someone else's job to do it. Don't let fear
of what they might think shut your life-giving testimony down. Don't
decide ahead of time that you could not or would not ever put someone
'on the spot' like that. Instead, cherish these precious seconds God gives
you with others—and be ready when those natural opportunities present
themselves—to share what Jesus has done for you. If you feel like you just
don't have a passion about sharing your faith with others, ask the Lord to

fill your heart with compassion for those who truly are at risk of spending eternity separated from God when their life here comes to an end. Ask God to put the kind of love in your heart for others that wants to see them thrive and live out their purpose here on earth—the kind of love that drives you to get out of your own comfort zone for someone else's sake.

You know what's crazy about all of it? We tend to get all uptight about this subject because we feel like it's all on us. But the truth is, it's not our job to "save" anyone. We don't even have the power to do that. It is the Holy Spirit who draws others to know Jesus and accept Him as their personal Savior. People come to know Jesus by what HE DID ON THE CROSS FOR THEM and by THE WORD OF OUR TESTIMONIES. The GOLD *we have to offer others* is to simply *share* what He's done for us! Simply GIVE THAT GIFT AWAY! Think of it like this. Remember each day that you have been given a 'platform'. Take on the mindset of giving away "your favorite things" when it comes to sharing the saving power of Jesus Christ everyday— "YOU can know Jesus! And YOU are getting Jesus! And YOU can know Jesus, too! We are all going to leave today KNOWING CHRIST PERSONALLY!" The gift of salvation truly is the gift that keeps on giving! Don't be a hoarder of your riches in Christ. Be sure to share that wealth with everyone. It truly is the best gift ever!

Lord, I want to pray boldly today that you will send me someone to share your saving grace with. I pray that you will replace my passivity with a passion to testify on behalf of all you've done for me. The saving of many is not up to me. But the sharing of Your love absolutely is. Replace my fear of sharing Jesus with an excitement to give away this amazing gift! I'm here, Lord. Yes, use me for your glory. Amen

THE MORE THE BETTER

DAY 36

"It's better to have a partner than go it alone. By yourself, you're
unprotected. With a friend you can face the worst. Can you round
up a third? A three-stranded rope isn't easily snapped."
ECCLESIASTES 4:9,12 THE MESSAGE

God places a high value on people. So, it should go without saying that He places a HIGH VALUE on relationships. In fact, our destiny is directly tied to our earthly relationships. In light of this truth, we should be aware that the enemy is working overtime to destroy all that God is building. And if he can't succeed at destroying these relationships, he counts on us being complacent within them.

Take a moment and think of someone who has made a significant
impact in your life.
Have you lost touch with them?
Do you need to thank someone for being a great friend?
Who have you been meaning to call but never get around to it?
Are you estranged from someone due to a challenging circumstance?

Has it been way too long since you reached out to a
particular family member?

Who is the Lord putting on your mind RIGHT NOW—that five minutes ago you might have resisted the urge to text them? You never know!
Taking a moment to reach out to someone God places on your heart may
be the answer to a prayer they've been petitioning for weeks. Through
the years, I've learned that we don't always have the next day to tell the
ones we love or miss that we appreciate them—or that we are sorry. Those
missed opportunities can leave deep scars and guilt in our hearts that
could have been avoided.

Rather than risking the disappointment of regret, take a moment to
write a note to a friend you appreciate. Send a text or email to someone
who you've lost touch with. Maybe consider calling a person that's now
estranged due to tough disappointments or a misunderstanding. Trust
that God DOES want your relationships to be strong and to thrive. Both
rekindling and revitalizing God-honoring relationships are SHINY steps
in the direction of loving people well. Don't let the enemy convince you
to be indifferent. He never has your best interest in mind. Instead, make
a move when you feel that nudge from the Lord. You have no idea of the
blessings that may await on the other side of your obedience! Go on!!
Throw a GOLD GLITTER BOMB in someone's direction! Somebody's
got to go first. We truly are better together.

*Heavenly Father, thank you for the people who have made a
positive impact on my life over the years. Bring specific individuals to my mind who need to hear from me personally. Forgive
me for the times I may have taken people for granted. Help me to
always honor those where honor is due—in ways that will bring
You glory above all else. Amen*

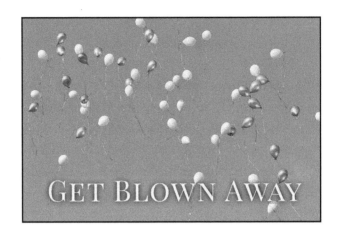

GET BLOWN AWAY

DAY 37

"God can do anything, you know—far more than you could ever imagine or guess or request in your wildest dreams! He does it not by pushing us around but by working within us, His Spirit deeply and gently within us. Glory to God in the church!"

EPHESIANS 3: 20-21 THE MESSAGE

id you know God has bigger dreams for you than you have for yourself? That's so exciting! Right? So how do you find out what that amazing destiny is? The answer is actually very simple although the follow through can sometimes feel like anything but easy. We can all get really attached to what we think we want or need. However, I've learned that one of the key principles to discovering God's amazing plan for our lives is more about detachment. What God is actually waiting on is for us to get out of our own way. And when I say "get out of our own way", I mean to be brave enough to clip the string on "how you think it should be" and letting that balloon fly. Many of us plan, dream and hustle toward a goal without ever even asking God if it fits into His perfect plan for us. How do I know that? Well, let's just say "I resemble that remark". Why? Because I am a dreamer. I believe in dreaming. And when I get excited about an idea, I'm floating "up, up and away" before I can even catch my breath! I'm writing things down. Calling a good friend. Researching every possibility that could come to life by birthing this amazing idea. But the thing that has left me 'deflated' every time is making the assumption that just because it's a good thing, it means it's the right thing for me.

Due to a new awareness of this pitfall, I'm learning to pause when great ideas come my way. I'm learning to seek God's opinion FIRST. Instead, I'm striving to know God better than the dreams I'm holding on to. He's taught me to understand that there is a 'NEVER' and an 'ALWAYS' within anything He calls us to do. Knowing these two things can help us gage our motives and our potential participation in everything that comes our way. The first is this: YOU AND I being "great" will NEVER be our purpose in life—because at the end of the day, our purpose is about something much bigger than us. The second follows with equal importance: helping a lot of people along the way will ALWAYS be at the root of our amazing destiny. Why? Because our whole existence revolves around others knowing the love of Jesus. Oh, and as a bonus, be ready for the character building that's coming along for the ride. It's a non-negotiable with God.

"God loves us too much to take us where our character can't hold us."

Robert Morris

And just in case you are wondering, this truth applies to ALL of us! If you are reading this devotional right now, I'm pretty sure you are still breathing. If you are still breathing, you are still on this earth. And if you are still on this earth, then God is not done with you yet! So don't make the mistake of "getting in your own way" by thinking that your time has passed in regards to God using you to accomplish something impactful for His Glory. Instead, get taken aback by the reality that God created you with a unique plan in mind along with a target group of people that your life will specifically impact. Furthermore, be ready to GET BLOWN AWAY by just how much you love it!! It's been eye-opening to witness

God's unique plans unfold in not only my life but others as well. He actually lines up for us what we would have chosen for ourselves if we'd had the ability to see the future through His eyes.

So, be open. Trust the process. You wait and see. Exciting days are ahead when you tether your hopes and dreams to the GOLD of God's sovereignty and let your ideas of what you thought it might be FLY! Wow! Take a look at that photo again. What a visual it is to imagine all of our dreams *collectively* submitted to God's plans. How about you? Are you in? I am! My balloon is the GOLD ONE on the far right. Which one is yours?

Dear Lord, thank you for giving me a specific destiny. Thank you for reminding me that if I'm still on earth, that you are not done with me yet. When I make my dreams all about me, I ask that you reign me back in quickly. When I get lazy and begin to believe the lies that I can do nothing that will be impactful, send me a reminder—through your Word or someone else—that inspires me to go for the GOLD you have set out for me. Be glorified in all that I put my hands to. It's in your precious name that I pray. Amen

THE GOLDEN RULE

DAY 38

"Don't pick on people, jump on their failures, criticize their
faults—unless, of course, you want the same treatment. That
critical spirit has a way of boomeranging. It's easy to see a smudge
on your neighbor's face and be oblivious to the ugly sneer on your
own. Do you have the nerve to say, 'Let me wash your face for
you,' when your own face is distorted by contempt? It's this whole
traveling road-show mentality all over again, playing a holier-
than-thou part instead of just living your part. Wipe that ugly
sneer off your own face, and you might be fit to offer a washcloth
to your neighbor"....
"Here is a simple, rule-of-thumb guide for behavior:
Ask yourself what you want people to do for you, then
grab the initiative and do it for them."
MATTHEW 7:1-5, 12 THE MESSAGE

It's a simple guide to behavior: Treat others the way you want to be treated. Chances are, you grew up calling it the "Golden Rule". Maybe you thought it was just a courteous way to live throughout your life. However, it's actually one of God's guidelines for living—that not only protects yourself and others—but also, if followed, keeps you from looking foolish to those around you.

I don't know about you, but it is very easy for me to not only recognize but also vocalize when someone is "petting my peeves". For many of us, it's easier to have an answer for how everyone else should behave, while being blind to our own shortcomings. Critical evaluations of others are quick to roll off our tongues while our precious egos tell us that "at least you're not as bad as that person". But lucky for me—and hopefully for you too—God's refining process won't let these habits go unchecked if you spend any time at all in His Word. My heightened awareness came when I asked the Holy Spirit to help me in this area. I'm hoping that some of the same cues that He's giving me will be impactful for you too.

I started by proactively asking the Lord to show me what it looks like to extend grace to others. He began reminding me of times when I was 'less knowledgeable about life decisions' so I could respond with encouragement rather than frustration when I see others falling short. I'm training my pride to stand down more often in order to see things from God's point of view rather than only from mine. And you know what? If I was to be completely honest with you, it has surprised me to notice how many times I've assumed the worst in someone's intentions rather than giving them the benefit of the doubt before I react. And for those who have meant intentional harm, He's allowed me to recognize the brokenness that lies behind their poor behavior which has enabled me to spend more time praying for them rather than spewing back hurt and anger in return.

But the greatest reminder from God has been that I can only control myself. And that every time I handle myself in a way that honors Him—no matter what others do—my actions make way for three outcomes that can't be undone. God gives me peace. He begins to de-escalate intense situations. And He replaces contempt with compassion. Ultimately, my obedience to follow God's instructions leaves an imprint of what Christ has done for me. Didn't God give us grace when we least deserved it? Wasn't He responding to us with love when we didn't even realize it? And didn't He follow through on goodness even when we weren't grateful?

My husband said it best when he responded to a comment made to him this week regarding his continued grace and participation in an environment that has seemed a little more 'self-serving' than what any of us would prefer for it to be. Her comment: "Wow, they seem to take advantage of you but I'm impressed that you still keep such a good attitude about it." His response: "Well, I don't do it for them."

Yep, that's the key. The Golden Rule is golden because when followed, it's more of a reflection of who God is than who we are. It tells more about our devotion to Him than it strokes our ego. It's really just evidence of Him purifying our hearts to resemble His never ending 24k status. I don't know about you, but my goal is to "STAY GOLD" like that.

Lord, help me to live out Your Word by adhering to the GOLDEN RULE. Give me the wisdom and discernment to respond to exhausting people and situations with Your supernatural grace. Thank you for first loving ME with that very same GOLD standard. Allow truth and kindness to be my goal as I interact with people each day. Help me to remember that reflecting You is the only true path to sincere humility and loving compassion. Amen

SHAKE OFF YOUR DUST

DAY 39

"Awake, Awake oh daughters of Zion; clothe yourself with
strength...shake off your dust; rise up, and sit enthroned...
free yourself from the chains on your neck."

ISAIAH 52: 1A-2 NIV

I can't imagine that there are many people reading this book that don't love a good "princess" story. I actually have a favorite fairytale in mind right now. It tells the story of an ordinary girl who finds out she has an extraordinary pedigree—which forces her to step into a destiny she never knew was hers. She's awkward and intimidated. At times, she is flat out rebellious when it comes to accepting her newfound role as a princess. But as the story unfolds, she begins to discover that the qualities she's needed to fulfill her destiny were within her all along. She realized her identity was grounded in who she actually was—not who she believed she was. In the end, she took her place on the throne, as we all hoped she would, and everyone lived happily ever after.

If it were only that simple. Right? Don't you wish solving our identity issues in life could be wrapped up in about 2 hours? We could laugh at ourselves most of the way through the process and end up rich and with a handsome prince gushing relentlessly at our feet. Most of us would jump on that narrative.

But what if it kind of was that simple? Well, minus the guaranteed riches and prince part. But what if a lot of our identity issues and our constant battles with insecurities are because we are looking at everything through the lens of who we *think* we are instead of "*Who's*" we actually are. If you came from an abusive family, then your title for yourself might be *abused*. Or, if you don't have a Division1 University to call your alma mater then you may have labeled yourself *less than*. Maybe you see *fat* when you look at yourself. Or, maybe it's *lonely*. Maybe it's *promiscuous*. Maybe it's *divorced*. It could be *childless*. You may see a *failure*. Maybe be *unloved*. For some, you may have labeled yourself *broken* because your identity is based on being the collateral damage of another's choices. But at the end of the day, these are circumstances or results from choices and actions. They don't define the inner core of who you are. And, I love that this scripture today tackles this head on.

You see, Israel had chosen just about everything BUT their identity in Christ. They chose idolatry, sexual sins, lack of follow through and flat out rebellion instead of living within the destiny God had for them as a people. They ended up suffering the consequences of their choices—-with innocent people suffering right along with the guilty. But in this passage, they had come to a place where it was time to come back to who they were. He tells them to awake and clothe themselves with strength. To shake off their dust and to rise up and sit enthroned. Wow! What a shout-out of redemption to embrace! It's interesting to note here too, even in the Greek translation, every one of those words follows very closely to our understanding of what they mean. In fact, to sit enthroned means to take a place of position. But the pivotal message in this scripture is where it reads: "Free yourself from the chains on your neck." When first reading it, I assumed that meant "get yourself out of your mess". If you do, then you can "sit enthroned." But through a deeper study of this passage, this is what I found:

The Pulpit Commentary states its explanation this way:
The Hebrew text reads: "The bands of thy neck are unloosened;" i.e.
I have caused thy chains to fall from thee - thou hast only to "rise," and
thou wilt find thyself free.

Do you need to read that again? Because this is pretty profound. After all the messes that God's people had caused, chosen or lived through, God is saying you aren't bound anymore. You are now being freed to move on. You just need to get up, to rise up, to clothe yourself with strength and move to the place you were destined to be. Who needs to be reminded that you are a daughter of the King of Kings? It doesn't matter if you feel worthy of the title. If you have accepted Jesus Christ as your personal Savior, that is "Who's" you are—and that is what defines you and your future. Not your past. Not even your present. If you choose to shake off your dust, rise up and take your place of position...the freedom to do that is already there. The chains are gone. You have been set free.

Maybe today, you're the gal, just like our princess—who's just an ordinary person—who finds out she has an extraordinary pedigree—which leads her to step into a destiny she never knew was hers. Beloved one, your identity is securely in Christ Jesus. So, what do you say? Once and for all. Awaken your heart to who you really are. Take hold of the strength that has been given to you. Shake off the dust from places and circumstances that sold you into slavery. Rise up and walk away from the way of life and "attached identities" that were never meant to be yours. Then sit enthroned with love and adoration for the One who set you free. And along the way, share your freedom story with all who will listen. Be watchful for someone who might be having their own identity crisis. Because anyone can find the dirt in someone else. We see it all of the time. As God's girls, let's be the ones who find the GOLD. Someone needs to know their crown is waiting for them.

Father, thank you that my identity in You overrides every careless decision I have ever made. I acknowledge that Your love for me covers a multitude of sins. I also love you for catching every tear I've cried over the heartbreaking consequences I have endured due to someone else's destructive choices. I believe that my future is in Your hands and that You have chosen to set me free from things that have held me hostage. May You be glorified as I position myself to rise up and be recognized as Yours—while simultaneously bowing down in adoration of my King. Amen

DAY 40

"The LORD your God is in your midst, a mighty one who will save; He will rejoice over you with gladness; He will quiet you by His love; He will exult over you with loud singing."

ZEPHANIAH 3:17 ESV

Many of us grow up doubting the love of God because we equate His love for us with relationships we have experienced here on earth. Broken vows, conditional loyalty or a lack of compassion from people we gave ours to—all taint our understanding of God's *unconditional* love for us. Even our own bad choices can cause us to doubt why God would choose to love us—no matter what. However, the reality of God's perfect and sacrificial love is IN OUR MIDST every day, whether we choose to acknowledge it or not. It is steadfast and unchanging. It also comforts and sustains. And when embraced, it compels us to love others the same way.

So, this week, take a few minutes to put a SPOTLIGHT specifically on God's love for you. Be awestruck by the fact that the God of the universe demonstrated the greatest act of love in the history of the world when He allowed His Son, Jesus Christ, to die on the cross just for us—despite our willful rebellion and rejection of this sacrificial gift. Even when we denied Him, He stood in the gap asking The Father to forgive us because we had no idea what we were actually doing. Take in this breathtaking truth for a moment. Have you ever stopped and acknowledged it? Have you let your guard down and professed your need for a Savior? Have you given His love a chance to change your life? If your answer is yes, then ask Him how you can put a spotlight on His priceless love as you come in contact with others each day. If you don't know Jesus as your personal Savior, there is no better time than this moment to recognize that He is IN YOUR MIDST and His life-giving LIGHT has fallen directly on YOU. God is for you and loves you more than you could ever imagine.

Before we go, indulge me here for just a second. Pretend you are basking in the spotlight featured in our photo. Think of His presence surrounding you like a shower of GOLD glitter. There is no way to escape it. You couldn't walk away untouched by it if you tried. There is no way you could leave that "scene" and not sparkle and shine. Now here is the reality. His love for YOU *is even greater than that.* His presence *even more intense.* His love isn't lackluster—it's extravagant! And the effects of embracing that love are no less evident to onlookers than being caught in that shower of gold glitter. Yes, linger a little while longer and keep a mental spotlight on that unbelievable love. Not a human's love that can come and go. God's love for you. He is IN YOUR MIDST desiring to shower you with His lavish love—in this moment, tomorrow's moments and every other moment to come.

You are not alone. You are dearly loved. And that reality does not change from day-to-day. It's not dependent on who you are, where you are or where you've been. Instead, it's a natural byproduct of who God is. Next time you hear the lyrics of a song beckoning ('with loud singing' as our scripture spoke of) to highlight 24k 'magic' in the air, quickly be reminded that you have the REAL DEAL. The God of the Universe is IN YOUR MIDST. Take it in, friend. It's 24k TRUTH! And yes, I'm with you. It's too powerful to ever *really* comprehend. But oh my goodness, let's spend a lifetime giving it a try.

Father God, how could it be that You, the God of the universe, are in my midst as I pray this prayer? The reality of it is almost too much for me to comprehend. Thank you for loving me. Thank you for setting me apart for your glory. Remind me throughout the day that You are right beside me. Show me specific people this week that I can shower with love—in the same way that You sacrificially love me. Amen

DAY 41

"If anyone thirsts, let him come to Me and drink."

JOHN 7:37 ESV

Have you ever had the thought: "I can't do this one more day"? Or "I can't take not knowing one more moment." I know I have. In fact, I had those exact statements come out of my mouth more times than I care to count—this month! Uggh.

Being able to experience peace of mind in the middle of a LONG journey is like a cool drink of water during a long trek across the desert. And if you are having some days like I've had, there are moments where I'm just parched. When you are sweaty, exhausted and feel like there should have been more than only 'sand' in sight at this point, it can get overwhelming. Many times the words that are quick to come from our mouths are: "I just don't know what to do!!" Or "If I just knew what to do to get out of this desert quicker, I would do it—but I don't know what to do!" But sometimes it's what God wants to accomplish in the desert that is slowing the progress down. The lessons and disciplines He is exposing us to are more important than our desired oasis. He is teaching me that rather than to focus on what I don't know to do, to instead focus on doing what I do know to do—dig a little deeper in our faith. Our pursuit of faith is the very process that actually strengthens our trust in a Holy God when our circumstances only look like shifting sand. That pursuit leads to the cool drink of water that will quench our thirst—even if it is just for the moment—and give us the stamina we need to continue the journey.

What does that look like? Literally, get up and do what you know to do. Open the "fridge" by opening God's Word. He's offering an ice-cold drink of water to quench your weary soul today. Sing a song of praise to remind yourself to be grateful. Wipe the sweat from your brow and start walking again. It's the only way you will get there. Sitting still and complaining of 'how hot it is' and mentally agonizing about 'how you still can't see your destination' will not get you any further along in your journey. Putting your feet, one in front of the other, is where forward progress becomes a reality.

And move forward with this in mind: You will need more than one drink of water along the way, right?? In fact, in order to survive the journey, you need constant drinks of water to stay hydrated and healthy—ready to take on the extremes that come on a long, hot, hard trek. If you choose not to drink, you basically choose to collapse. It's that simple. So it is with us. Listening to Worship music refreshes us. Reading God's Word re-hydrates us—just like crying, complaining and refusing to take the "drinks of fresh water" you need will *dehydrate* you. At the end of the day, meditating and professing His promises produces a "winner" mentality—which is the mindset you need to finish well.

So, do what you know to do today. Drink from the living water and expand your faith. Give your spiritual body the same thing your physical body needs to function optimally—fresh gulps of living water—like you were drinking from a water hose on a hot day! Hey, "hydration" is key for our physical bodies! Take on that same mentality in your spiritual life as well and get ready to be amazed at the benefits that await you. You'll find your doubt in a drought—and your faith drenched in the gold of God's truth.

One day in the future, when asked about your situation, your response will not be, "Whew, as I look back, I have no idea how I made it". Instead, it will be, "I know exactly what I did to survive while I was in the desert. May I share it with you?" And friend, that will be the GOLD you can give to another worn out and thirsty soul. Until then, GUZZLE God's Word every chance you get.

Lord, help me to focus on the things I can control in times that are exhausting and uncertain. I know that Your Word offers that tall drink of water I so desperately need when I'm parched. Yet, so many times I refuse that spiritual hydration for my thirsty soul. Forgive me for that, Father. Thank you for providing what I need as I go through life's trials. When I'd rather spend my time complaining that I'm 'thirsty', please remind me to take a drink of Your living water instead. Amen

DAY 42

"Do you not know that your bodies are temples of the Holy Spirit,
who is in you, whom you have received from God?
You are not your own; you were bought at a price.
Therefore, honor God with your bodies."

1 CORINTHIANS 6:19-20 NIV

Sometimes, a gal can start reading her Bible with no idea that God is about to rock her world. How do I know that? Because, one morning, it happened to me. After years of reading this verse in Corinthians, The Lord gave me an eye-opening analogy along with a fresh perspective that I believe is worth sharing with you. Until this particular encounter, my basic understanding of the passage was "God is with you always"—so don't do things you wouldn't do in front of Him. Don't eat or drink anything that would "dishonor your temple". Don't smoke. Don't have sex outside of marriage. You get the gist—don't do anything you wouldn't be comfortable doing with or in front of Jesus. I am in agreement with that insight to this day. But one morning, a different line within the verse came leaping off the page: "You were bought at a price". The Holy Spirit used a challenging set of circumstances—leasing a house when we were so ready to own a home—to unveil a much needed lesson. Let me explain.

When leasing a house, though you may reside there, typically you aren't allowed to make any changes. There is no knocking down walls, changing out fixtures or replacing floors and countertops. The appliances stay in place and the cabinets don't get a fresh coat of paint. It doesn't matter how great your vision is for "what it could be." The decisions aren't yours to make. However, what if the circumstances changed and you were to purchase the house you are in? Once you close on the deal, it is your property to improve upon. Any area that you choose to make changes in, well, you now have the authority to do them. You can demolish anything that gets in the way of your plans of making the house your home. So, as the new owner, you go to work.

But what if at that point, the prior owner came in and said, "Hey, I don't want you to do that! I liked it the way it was! I always loved that shade of blue on my walls. That was my favorite room! You can't change that!" What would you be thinking at that moment? Probably…your first thought would be, "TOO BAD"! However, your *actual* response back might be, "I have a vision for this home now that I own it. Once we closed on the deal and I received the keys, you gave up ownership and any future decision making in this project." And that would be perfectly reasonable, right?

Well know this. That is the same way God feels about us. Once we accept Him as our personal Savior, we can't keep holding onto ownership of our lives. There comes a point where we should acknowledge our lives have been bought at a price and we aren't the "owners" anymore—that we surrendered the keys to our life when we accepted what Christ did for us on the cross. He has a beautiful design in mind for our lives. But it will include demolition in some areas. Walls in our hearts and minds will have to be knocked down along with adding some new fixtures that bring 'better light' to previously dark spaces. If you have accepted Jesus as your Savior, you've been bought for a price. He has paid for your life in full. He is not 'leasing you'—He's now the rightful new owner.

So, let Him do His work without attempting to block His plan. Make room for the overall vision He has for your life. He has a great "knack" for taking a mess and transforming it into a masterpiece. He is the ultimate "fixer-upper"! Though you may not understand the future beauty that awaits as He makes these changes that seem to leave nothing but wreckage and dust behind, be assured in the end you will stand in awe of what He knew you could be the whole time. Don't make the mistake of trusting Chip and Joanna Gaines more than you trust God. When they start a project, we never worry about the outcome! We have faith in their abilities! We trust it will be stunning! So, TRUST GOD LIKE THAT! Surrender the vision you have for your life to the best "INTERIOR" DESIGNER—ever. He's got this, friend. What He is about to do in you will make you—and everyone else looking on—squeal with delight and amazement. Just so you know, I personally can't wait for Him to open up these GOLDEN GATES so we all can see the "big reveal". It's going to be FABULOUS!

Father, I'm sorry that I sometimes forget the "cost" that was involved in ensuring I could have unbroken fellowship with you. You paid a very high price so that I could be Yours—yet much of the time, I hold on to the keys of my heart as if you have no right to them and convince myself that You don't have the authority to make any changes that I don't "approve of". Please forgive me. Move right on in. Make yourself at home. I can't wait to see what You do with the 'place'. Amen

APPLES OF GOLD
IN SETTINGS OF SILVER

DAY 43

"Timely advice is lovely, like gold apples in a silver basket."

PROVERBS 25:11 *NLT*

I have a question for us today. How shiny are our words? If others were taking note, what would they hear? Are they bringing healing or showing frustration? Are they received like a precious gift or blasted from our keyboards like a destructive bomb? Your words can bring nourishment to your family and friends' emotional health like apples bring nourishment to their bodies. Would others say they are 'malnourished' or 'satisfied' due to what you say or don't say? And what about the delivery of those words? How things are said can change the whole way in which they're received! My mom has cautioned me many times: "Honey, you are right...but it's your tone you need to work on". Do you ever have that issue as well?

It is also very important to remember that just because you are thinking it, doesn't mean you have to say it out loud—especially when you are frustrated. We have all heard that we should "count to 10" before we say something to our kids. But what about our spouses, our parents, a co-worker, a friend? It's both baffling and disappointing that our human nature finds it so easy to use 'our most careless words' when speaking to the people we love the most. To be honest, sometimes we give more courtesy to a perfect stranger! And the social media world... sadly, it's become a filterless free for all! As a society, we have somehow adopted the belief that it is our duty to call people out PUBLICLY...even though it's hurtful. So today, let's focus on being more careful with our words. In fact, let's ask ourselves these questions BEFORE we speak:

Is this the right time to have this conversation?
Does what I'm about to say bring a constructive solution to this verbal exchange or is it a means to get my frustration out?
Would I want someone to repeat what I'm about to say?
Will my input add value to this conversation?
Does this interaction build a deeper trust with the person I'm speaking with?

Remember these cues next time your emotions get ready to take a hard right turn instead of heading down the straight and narrow path God has set out for us. You know, "If Momma ain't happy—ain't nobody happy" is no badge of honor to wear in your home. Harsh words spoken due to our 'bad moods' breed resentment in our families and they're also eventually mimicked by our kids and grandkids. Instead, make sure you're leaving behind a trail of gold and not coal. The gold will add value to the lives of those you love. The coal—well, it leaves a heck of a mess to clean up later. Why add that task to your already long to-do list? Yep, that's what I thought, too.

Let's go for the apples of GOLD! Let's make sure we are using these settings of silver (our communication devices) to build up instead of tear down, sister. Let's use the most powerful tool we own—our mouths—to make our world a little more SHINY... each and every day.

Heavenly Father, it's so easy to say what is on my mind when I'm frustrated. The problem is that those harsh words are impossible to take back once I do. I want to live out my faith by first cleaning up my excuses—for allowing an unbridled tongue to run wild when I'm upset. Lord, will you forgive me? Help me to treat others the way I would want to be treated. When my mouth or my typing fingers go in motion, I pray that grace will abound instead of harsh comments. Amen

GETTING GOLD STARS

DAY 44

"Let us not neglect our church meetings, as some people do,
but encourage each other, especially now that the day
of His coming back again is drawing near."

HEBREWS 10:25 TLB

Many people today are buying into the misconception that our faith is between us and God—a private affair that is no one else's business. If this is you, I'd like for you to reconsider your stance on this subject. Through studying God's Word, it's clear that we are not meant to do a "spiritual journey" on our own. We were created to be together. Our hearts were designed to be strengthened when we allow ourselves to connect with others who are seeking to experience God's power and plan for their lives as well. Attending a local church service is a vital step in seeing this divine connection flourish.

However, there is one obstacle to overcome—one undeniable truth you can't glaze over—which is this: THERE IS NO PERFECT CHURCH. And why do we know that? Because there is one common denominator in EVERY church that will keep it imperfect—and that is people. Where people are, imperfection will always exist.

And to further complicate things, we have also adopted a misconception that continues to undermine the priority of church attendance in our culture today. You see, many of us have been raised to believe that church is 'something we do' instead of 'who we are'. That it's a building holding some sort of reverence and that by going there, we get a 'gold star' for our efforts. But in reality, the most important part of a church is not the bricks and mortar—it is the people inside that building. It's pretty easy to connect the dots when you think about it. If there are no people, there is no church.

It's also tempting to conclude that every church is basically the same. So, if we had a bad experience at one, then all churches must be bad and not worth attending. Has that ever happened to you? Were you hurt, overlooked or even taken advantage of last time you attended...BY PEOPLE?

Or instead, you may be generally thinking, "I have been to a lot of churches and I have never been happy with any of them." If so, may I be a little bold and point out the obvious? The common denominator in that scenario—well, that is you. I don't say that to offend anyone. But I do say it to encourage you to reconsider your decision to give up on church as a whole. God's plan is to use His church to save the world. And just so you know—there is no 'back-up' plan. In light of that truth, don't be tempted to let your prior experiences with "church"—the ones that may have left a bad taste in your mouth—keep you stuck in a place of spiritual isolation which is both detrimental to you and the many people your life could have a positive effect on. What a costly consequence that would be for everyone involved!

Today's challenge is simple. Plan to attend a service at a local Bible-believing church of your choice this week. Not because it will get you favor with God—because we don't earn that by simply showing up. And don't go to check off a virtual box that makes you feel better—because if that's the case, then again, you are missing the point. That's just chasing pointless gold stars. Instead, gather together with a community of believers that will usher in the opportunity to be blessed, equipped, challenged, and encouraged. Worship with a group of people who share the same desire you have—which I pray is to receive a broader understanding of the love of Christ. You'll find yourself wondering why you ever settled on going in order to get a "gold star" when you start leaving with "gold nuggets" from His Word that will change your life FOREVER—and potentially every life *your* life touches too.

Dear God, help me to remember that no matter how messy the dynamics of church can be at times, it's still part of YOUR PLAN for us as believers. Let me never forget that YOU are actually the only GOLD STAR that is ever worth pursuing. Give me a love for people and a desire to serve them that can only come from you. Lead me to areas within the church that need my gifts and talents so I can be a contributing factor to the local church's success. I want to always be a light that helps your message be illuminated in a world that needs You so desperately—just like I do. Amen

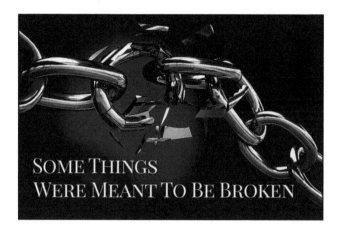

SOME THINGS WERE MEANT TO BE BROKEN

DAY 45

"The Lord is close to the broken-hearted and saves those who are crushed in spirit"

PSALM 34:18 NIV

When I saw this picture of a broken chain, I couldn't help but ponder about things that are broken. Truth is, the concept of something being "broken" usually always has a negative connotation. And for good reason! When making my list it was easy to see that certain things were NOT "meant to be broken". On that list were things like eye glasses, bones, one's spirit, cars, toys, fingernails, promises or our hearts. When something breaks that was intended to stay intact in order to be used, it has no other outcome than disappointment, frustration and most likely being thrown away.

However, it was interesting to find that when I made my list of things that WERE meant to be broken, it was actually much longer than the first one!! But what was most interesting is that every single thing that was *destined to break* produced a beneficial, and more often than not, a joyful outcome as a result of the breaking. Check out just a few of the things that made my list:

Broken Stereotypes bring acceptance.
Broken glow sticks bring light.
A fever that is broken brings healing.
A horse that's been broken brings transportation.
Broken water balloons bring laughter.
Broken bread brought fellowship.
A news story, once broken, brings information.
A broken glass ceiling brings opportunity.
A bad habit that is broken brings peace.
And a broken egg, well, it brings forth valuable nutrition.

Many of you reading this today could be going through a season of pressing or what feels like a full-on crushing. As you look around, you may feel there is no hope—that everything seems broken—with no recovery in sight. During these challenging times all dreaming, hope, joy and vision can be squeezed from our line of sight. But I would like to encourage you today that if the Lord has allowed a season of brokenness in your life, that He always has a good result or outcome waiting on the other side.

Jesus, our example to live by, knew fully what it was to endure suffering. He, like us, even asked the Lord if He could "let this cup pass" so He would not have to walk through this unthinkable hurt. In fact, he didn't just ask once, He asked three times. He was so anguished that He actually sweat drops of blood over his circumstances. However, the words that followed His original request to skip "the assignment" were this: "Nevertheless, not my will but Yours be done." (Matthew 26:42 NIV) God used His broken body to save mankind for all eternity. Though no one watching could see or understand the good, it did not change the fact that God was working out and fulfilling the miracle He promised generations before Him. And Jesus's real life example of obedience and submission to God's will opened the doors of heaven for every future generation to come.

I don't share these words lightly—AT ALL. Broken places are painful at best and excruciating more times than not. But I encourage you to not only believe in God's love for you but to seek His perspective on your pain as you walk through a place of brokenness. Could He use your circumstances to usher in acceptance? To bring forth light where there has previously been darkness? Is there an opportunity that can be found? Is there a new place for fellowship with someone? Can sensitive information now be shared that may not have been possible before this time? Is there spiritual nutrition and peace that are yours now for the taking that you didn't see previously? Can you even find inexplicable joy—maybe ever laughter—that comes from pressing into Jesus as you persevere? God loves you so much. In fact, He loves you no less than He loved His only Son. Trust that if He has called "it" to be broken, that He has claimed "it" to become a new way to bring Him Glory. May The Living God bind your heart with His as we believe and internalize the passage we began with. Hold fast sweet one. Help is on the way.

Father God, only you know what things in my life must be broken in order to bring forth new life. When things seem to be 'falling apart', give me the supernatural ability to look at my circumstances with anticipation of the good to come—rather than be convinced that the breaking was never a part of your plan. You knew my path in life before I ever took a breath. Give me the kind of peace that only comes from knowing You so I can stay the course. I want my testimony to be used for your glory. I'm going to say it over and over again until I believe it in my core: "You can be trusted, Lord. You WILL be found faithful." Amen

THE MIX UP

DAY 46

"This book of the law shall not depart from your mouth, but you
shall meditate on it day and night, so that you may be careful to
do according to all that is written in it;
for then you will make your way prosperous,
and then you will have success."

JOSHUA 1:8 ESV

In the past few years, the Lord has given me a heightened sensitivity to the watering down of—if not complete change of—the authentic Word of God. Using the power of social media, people are presenting beautiful posts featuring parts of scripture references mixed in with their own wisdom in an attempt to spoon feed us spiffy quotes of motivation to live by. And whether they are 'intending to deceive' or just don't even realize what they are doing, we are falling hook, line and sinker for poor counsel. In order to give you a taste of what seems to be a growing problem, I've rewritten a familiar scripture passage in what might be considered the "world's point of view". It came out a little something like this:

"Try to be strong and courageous—but if you get unsure, go ahead and freak out! Embrace who you really are. No one can tell you how to feel. And when it comes to God's commands and guidelines, only worry about doing the things you feel like doing. It's your life to live after all. Try every direction your feelings lead you down because there is no way to know if you will be successful anyway—so try everything and see what sticks! Oh, and regarding the Bible being a current standard to live by, it was written a long time ago for people a long time ago. Don't worry about meditating on it day and night....it will wear you out! It might even put you to sleep! No one REALLY DOES what it says anyway. There might be some good suggestions. But if you want to be prosperous, do whatever it takes! If you want to be successful, it's up to you! No one knows what you need more than you do—so just trust your gut feelings on everything. They will never let you down. And listen again: "command- shamand"...I mean really! Everyone freaks out! Don't beat yourself up! We are on our own here at the end of the day! And life can be scary with a lot of uneasiness. So, don't wait! Go out there and get yours! It's yours to take on your timeline. Whenever YOU are ready, go figure it out! You've got this babe! Oh, and good luck!"

Sound familiar? Has some of that advice been given to you before? Have you given that advice yourself recently? If you aren't in the Bible regularly, you might have read that and had no idea that it was linked to scripture at all. If you have been studying a while, did you recognize the scripture but also recognize the world's view mixed into it? Either way, let's take a look at what Joshua 1:7-11 actually says:

"Only be strong and very courageous, being careful to do according to all the law that Moses my servant commanded you. Do not turn from it to the right or to the left, that you may have good success wherever you go. This Book of the Law shall not depart from your mouth but you shall meditate on it day and night, so that you may

be careful to do according to all that is written in it. For then you will make your way prosperous, and then you will have good success. Have I not commanded you? Be strong and courageous. Do not be frightened, and do not be dismayed, for the Lord your God is with you wherever you go." And Joshua commanded the officers of the people, "pass through the midst of the camp and command the people: 'prepare your provisions, for within three days you are to pass over this Jordan to go in to take possession of the land that the Lord your God is giving you to possess."

Well. I think we can easily agree that there are quite a few discrepancies between the two passages. What a difference it would have made for the Israelites to have followed the "world's advice" over the divine instructions that would guide them from the wilderness to the Promised Land. The lesson for all of us? That deadly cocktail of mixing God's Word and the world's advice could be keeping you and me from moving forward into God's 'promised land' for us—where we'll thrive and find joy and purpose like we never knew we could! But the only way to know if you are following the world's point of view or God's Word is by being in the pages of your Bible enough to know the difference. Girl, you've got to read your Bible—regularly!! And on top of that, let's get more intentional about asking the Holy Spirit to help us recognize when we're subtly internalizing information that will ultimately take us off course. Lastly, don't be tempted to change God's wisdom to suit your own. Don't try and bring God down to your level of thinking. Instead, let His Word drive you to new levels of obedience!

In a world that constantly encourages us to let our feelings boss us around, let's give scripture that position of authority instead. Don't get "mixed up" on what to trust. It's high time we let the GOLD of God's Word get BAKED into our psyches—not a bunch of social media hype. God has the recipe for success that is "fool-proof" every time. And yes. Using that term was definitely intentional. I figured we could handle the 24k truth.

God, YOUR WORD IS TRULY GOLD. How could I ever fall into the trap of chasing after another's counsel? But yet, it happens all the time. Lord, please give me the wisdom to see the difference between the real thing and a fake. Show me when to close my eyes and cover my ears. Stir a love for your teachings so deeply in my heart that I crave it over anything else that wants to tickle my fancy. I never want to be mixed up—just shored-up in the wisdom that can only come from spending time in my Bible. Amen

NEVER LATE

DAY 47

"But those who hope in the LORD will renew their strength.
They will soar on wings like eagles; they will run and
not grow weary; they will walk and not grow faint."

ISAIAH 40:31 NIV

Have you ever felt like God was playing hide and seek with you just when you need Him most? Or, maybe you have felt God has ignored your desperate pleas for help. I understand those feelings. But no matter what it looks like, God is not playing a game of hide and seek with you. He has not chosen to desert you either. It's all just a matter of timing. His to be exact.

When God is running just a little bit behind in our eyes, our temptation is to give up or try to take matters into our own hands. The problem is, both are contradictory actions to experiencing God's best. The enemy wants to distract you and make you believe that it's all up to you. That if you don't act, all will be lost. But, let's not forget, he is also a liar. Yeah, there's that. So, let me hit you with a question the Holy Spirit has asked me once or twice: "If you think God's best is taking a long time, don't you think it will take even longer if He has to keep stopping to clean up your "oh, I'm sorry, you were right, I should have waited" little messes before finishing His process?" There is nothing ultra-spiritual about the question. It's kind of common sense—and I tend to be a girl who can be reasoned with if you come at me with the obvious. What about you?

My sweet Daddy has always reminded me of this when patience was hard to muster and I wanted to give up on trusting God's timing: "Sweetie, God's timing is perfect. He's never late. The only problem is, He's never early, either." Ok, Daddy. You may be right, but it's still frustrating, isn't it? Nevertheless, it does beg us to look up the word perfect. If His timing is perfect, what can we expect?

Perfect: without flaws, defects or shortcomings; conforming absolutely to the description or definition of an ideal; excellent or complete beyond practical improvement; exactly fitting the need in a certain situation or for a certain purpose; accurate, exact, or correct in every detail; thorough to a tee; totally pure in every way

Looking at that definition of 'perfect' encourages me to want to wait on God's best. When I think of how many times I have gotten ahead of Him and the results that I experienced because of that—this definition QUICKLY reminds me that I'd rather wait for His perfect timing. Our human minds and our rebel wills argue that we think we know what is best. However, we have no idea of the things that God knows. So, to know that His perfect timing could be stated more like "excellent or complete beyond practical improvement" timing or "correct in every detail" timing. Wow, I know there is a huge chance if I get ahead of God, I definitely won't be experiencing a whole lot of that.

So today, let's take a step back and meditate on trusting God's 'perfect' timing. The kind of time that only God can tell. Truth be told, as agonizing as waiting can be, you and I would most likely agree on this: The day before He moves, you feel like you can't bear one more moment of waiting. The day after the day He moves, you can't feel anything but praise and thanksgiving. The rest of it just becomes a memory. So, may I encourage you with something a good friend said to me in a time of desperate waiting.

"Don't let too much, too long, too hard, or too late hinder you progress."

Debbie Stuart

Hey, it's going to be 'eagle wing mounting' time before you know it! For now, just be still and know that He is God. Ask Him, who gives generously, for more strength when you are feeling weak or faint. You won't be disappointed if you do. Focus on His goodness and His character. In fact, in this moment, whisper out loud to the Lord: "You're never going to let me down." Maybe you need to whisper it several times. Because, that is SOLID GOLD TRUTH my friend. He's never going to let us down. He is only going to exceed our expectations.

Lord, thank you that my lack of understanding Your timing does not negate the perfection of it. Help me to align my emotions and my actions with the truth of Your Word. My job is to trust in You with all of my heart and acknowledge your Lordship over everything. Then I can rest in knowing that I'm moving toward your best. Amen

DAY 48

"Now to Him who is able to do immeasurably more than all we ask or imagine, according to His power that is at work within us, to Him be glory in the church and in Christ Jesus throughout all generations, forever and ever! Amen."

EPHESIANS 3:20-21 NIV

Have you ever been in a situation and thought, why me God? Has that same situation ever made you start to grow seeds of resentment toward others who you thought could have prevented it? Maybe you have deep regrets that cause you to self-loathe. Or, maybe it's something that has taken you by surprise and it has you questioning God's love for you. Many of us, if we were honest, have wondered why a loving God would allow difficulties to exist that are so painful that they crush your spirit to the point of despair. My guess is that if we were having coffee together right now, you could share a story or two with me—and me with you. But how *should* we cope in these moments? Part of my personal refinement has been to learn the art of reframing.

I'm thankful that God gives us people to learn from—living examples of what to do in times like these. He also instructs us clearly in His Word. On top of that, there are worship songs filled with truth about reframing our circumstances. But today, I have the privilege of sharing a tiny version of a huge testimony wherein the "reframing" of someone's conversations with God completely changed the outcome of their circumstances.

A woman I know was facing an extremely tough surgery after months of chronic pain in her mouth. A bone spur had developed in her jaw that was affecting her ability to talk and eat—both being almost unbearably painful to do at times. The osteoporosis she had been managing for years was not only exacerbating the situation, it was also a factor that had to be taken into consideration as decisions were made on how to treat this excruciating problem. At 76 years old, this beautiful woman of faith was racked with fear and beginning to feel some of the very feelings we discussed at the opening of our conversation today.

While showering one morning, the Holy Spirit prompted her to pray and ask God to release her from her fear—not the situation—but from her fear of the situation. As she prayed, lessons from others, promises from God's Word and reminders of truths she had been taught over the years began to remind her that we are here for God's glory. She asked for God to use her circumstances for His glory. That He would replace her fear with courage—and that others would see Him in her as she trusted Him with this difficult situation. She asked for forgiveness for the bitterness that had been taking root in her heart over having to walk the path ahead and then asked Him to change her attitude of resentment into one of thanksgiving instead. The prayers were not only heartfelt but sincere—and they moved the heart of God. This is how I know.

As she was walking out of the shower, she could literally feel the weight of the fear being lifted from her. It was a feeling of release that was unexplainable. In fact, there was such a noticeable difference that she became overwhelmed with thanksgiving—enough that she had to lay prostrate in her closet in order to *actually* bow down and thank God for taking her fear away and replacing it with courage. As she thanked Him, her offering of praise continued to resound, "Be glorified in my life Lord. In every part. Through everything. Be Glorified in me." So amazing, right? What a gift to be relieved from the fear that had been tormenting her!

She got up from the closet floor, renewed in spirit, and walked toward the laundry room—basically moving on with her day as she embraced the new courage God had given her. All of the sudden, she felt a strange sensation in her jaw that made her stop in her tracks. As she stood still to figure out what was going on, she felt something loose in the back of her mouth. At first thought, she was afraid the dying bone in her jaw had caused her to lose a tooth. Concerned, she reached into her mouth to pull out whatever was lying at the back of her gum line. Do you know what she pulled out? It was not a tooth. Shockingly, it was the bone spur itself. The culprit. The source of her agony. The reason behind her need for surgery. The very root of her pain was now in the palm of her hand—literally. Not only was it removed, there was no evidence it had ever been there. No broken gum line, no blood, no pain. The dentist and surgeon went on to confirm: God performed an unexplainable miracle.

Why do you think I wanted to share this story with you? We might be tempted to assume the focus should be on the excitement of God "removing" her painful situation. And why wouldn't we! That is not only amazing but a beautiful gift as well. But the real power in this story began when she *reframed* who the story is actually about. Everything that touches us here on earth is an avenue to see God's glory revealed. When God moves, it's always with that in mind. When we reframe our circumstances as avenues for God's glory to be revealed, it shifts not only our perspective but then our emotions as well. Before you know it, trust begins to follow suit.

I'm realizing fear, anxiety and frustration come when I view my life as mine—*my* circumstances, *my* hurt, *my* needs, or *my* disappointment. But when I reframe my story, I understand that instead of making it *my story* that God needs to show up and play a part in, I'm learning to ask for help in the moment—so that I can be a good steward of HIS STORY THAT I PLAY A PART IN. When that refinement takes place and accomplishes its work, that is when the miracles start taking place. Fear loses its grip—not only because God promises that He will never leave us nor forsake us, but because we also have the assurance that He will accomplish His best for us at the EXACT MOMENT that gives Him the most glory—period.

No, there is nothing too impossible for our God. Just ask my precious Mom. She was the recipient of that miracle. I only wish you could hear her tell the story. The awe in her voice and the passionate words that fall from her lips are a natural result of trusting God IN EVERY WAY SHE KNEW HOW—and watching Him come through for her in ways she could not have dreamed to tell. But it started with the simple reframing of her perspective on who her story is actually about.

Can I leave you with the question the Lord asked me this morning? "LeeAnn, if someone was to look at a framed picture of your life circumstances, who do they see—Me or you?" Personally, it was a sobering moment as I bowed my head to answer the Lord honestly and sincerely. Sweet friend, ask God to be glorified in your circumstances. Ask Him for the courage to trust Him with everything you've got. Take time to put a GOLD FRAME around *the real face of the story*. Have the grace and humility to give Him the lead role—so that the standing ovation is directed to The Worthy One when the curtain falls on the chapter you're currently living out.

> *Lord, help me to remember that You are the author, star and finisher of my story. If I don't have that straight in my mind, so much unneeded anxiety is sure to follow. Be magnified in jaw-dropping ways so that all who are watching me will instead be drawn to You. The Bible promises that You will not leave me nor forsake me. Help me to live like I believe those words of TRUTH—because I know that's the key to You remaining glorified in my life. Amen*

DAY 49

"They followed a daily discipline of worship in the Temple
followed by meals at home, every meal a celebration,
exuberant and joyful, as they praised God."

ACTS 2:46 THE MESSAGE

What makes a happy meal? It's not just a tagline made famous by a well-known fast food restaurant! It's a lot more than cheeseburgers, fries and a coke. A "HAPPY MEAL" is one shared around the table with others. Where conversation is encouraged. Laughter ignited. And quality time together is prioritized—with EVERYONE unplugging from EVERYTHING else that vies for their attention each day.

Unfortunately, busy schedules, electronic devices and television screens are stealing our daily opportunities to bond as families. We're being tempted to believe that a device-free dinner gathered around an actual table isn't important anymore...that it's old-fashioned. However, it cannot be denied that we live in a time where disconnection within families is at an all-time high. And as I read the articles and statistics that support that reality, I can't help but wonder if much of it could be avoided by resetting some basic priorities.

Life IS busy, especially when we're "chasing" kids. We raised four ourselves!! But some of our lack of "family time" has become non-existent because of pure laziness on our part. It's just easier to let everyone do their own thing. In fact, many empty nesters, with no one's schedule to manage, choose to sit in a chair in front of the television and eat their dinner—never saying a word to each other. To further make a point, how many times have you witnessed a couple in a restaurant sitting across from each other at a table, never saying a word? Why? Because one or both of them have their eyes locked in on a phone screen instead of each other!

Can we pause here a minute? How many meaningful conversations are being lost? How many opportunities have we missed to affirm each other or our children—instead, allowing the "world" to do it for us? Meals enjoyed together are a great place to invite others into our daily lives. Around a table, you get a window into areas that may need your attention as a parent or a spouse. Think about this. How many times would actual eye contact with the people we love—and who love us—give a weary soul that's worked all day the opportunity to be validated and appreciated? (Whether that work be outside or inside the home.) Maybe we might learn a little more about someone we thought we knew so well. Not to mention, this is a time where young children learn table manners, the art of conversation and the opportunity to show gratitude and thanksgiving for the blessings of everyday provision in their lives.

Jesus, himself, modeled the importance of having meals together throughout His life here on earth. There was a wedding in Cana where he turned water into wine. There was the dinner with Zaccheus the tax collector. There was that time where the woman used her perfume to wash Jesus' feet while a group of people were relaxing around the table. And we all know of the Last Supper where Jesus enlightened his disciples on the life changing events that were about to take place in His life and theirs. He showed us that sharing a meal not only connects us with others, it gives us opportunities to break down barriers that threaten our unity. He used times of eating with others as an occasion to honor their gifts. And His "dinner dates" taught us how to bless our friends and family and sometimes "solve the world's problems" over a hot meal. All throughout His time here on earth, He demonstrated that shared meals around tables were for the purpose of bringing people together.

Although this "ancient practice" of eating together at the table is threatened with a chance of extinction, we CAN change this trend! Whether it's take-out, a sandwich or a crockpot dinner, put it on a plate—even if it's a paper one—and eat it at the table TOGETHER. That's right! Gather'em all up and say, "Dinner's on the table!", and insist they sit down and dine together. THEN DO THE UNTHINKABLE, and turn the TV OFF! (Next, ignore the eye rolling. They'll thank you later.) Moms of preschoolers, I encourage you to sit down with your little ones and eat lunch. Don't use that time to "keep them distracted' while you do something else. Sing silly songs and make them laugh. Teach them table manners and make it fun! And by all means, let's ALL set some "device" boundaries at dinner time! Take a 30 minute break and be completely present for conversations over dinner. Let's put the "HAPPY" back in our meals. Oh, but with one stipulation! Don't forget a GOLDEN RULE in regards to our dining etiquette: No elbows on the table, please. Bon Appetit'!

Lord, thank you for the many ways you provide for our well-being. I pray that dinner time will become dedicated to honoring what you have done in our lives. A time we could celebrate each other, talk about our wins, pray for each other's needs and be able to give thanks for all of the provisions that are so easily taken for granted each day. Help me to troubleshoot in the areas where life gets in the way of this commitment. Give me creative solutions for implementing this important task when it seems impossible to accomplish. Please stir this same desire in the hearts of my family members as we commit to this precious time together. Amen

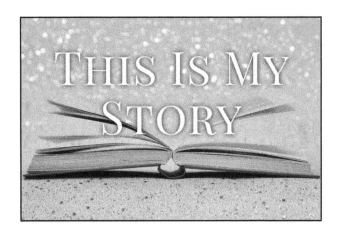

DAY 50

*"Instead, you must worship Christ as Lord of your life. And if
someone asks about your hope as a believer, always be ready
to explain it. But do this in a gentle and respectful way. Keep
your conscience clear. Then if people speak against you,
they will be ashamed when they see what a good life
you live because you belong to Christ."*

1 PETER 3:15-16 NLT

The focus of our last day together is wrapped around the power of
our story. And though we have touched on this subject in previous
weeks, today's focus is coming from yet a different angle! Personally, it is
probably the most tender of any subject that I have written so far. Why,
because our stories are, well—SO PERSONAL! If you're like me, there are
pieces and twists to your story where disappointment and regret feel like
the only narrative. It can be overwhelming to even think of sharing those
places of vulnerability. But let me encourage you with something the Lord
has *burned* (maybe I should say "refined"...all I know is that it was mighty
HOT and UNCOMFORTABLE at times) into the very fabric of my being:
When God asks us to share our stories, it's always with a KINGDOM
PURPOSE in mind.

Those of us who have experienced 'the grace that's greater than all of our sins' can be strengthened in knowing that Romans 8:28 promises us we have a Savior who does not waste anything. In fact, the very thing that you thought might kill you gives you "24k street cred" with another person who is walking with the same heartbreak. I have even found over the years that God literally orchestrates windows of opportunity where our life experiences are the very avenues that give us the ear of someone who may not have otherwise opened up to us. However, *also over the years*, God has revealed TWO hurdles that can sometimes hinder our ability to convey our stories *effectively*: TOO LITTLE and TOO MUCH. So can we take a moment to dive a little deeper into the delicate framework of actually sharing your testimony?

When you feel prompted to share your story, don't presume that this automatically means you are to go out and share EVERY DETAIL of your story with EVERYONE. There are things that we submit to the Lord, where He allows it to be shared only with Him. HOWEVER, I am encouraging you in this: If you're sitting across from a woman and everything in you is screaming, "if I don't open up and share more of my story in this moment God has given me, we're going to lose her"—then by all means, SHARE. If her loss of hope is crushing her view of what God can redeem in her circumstances, please don't hold back your life-giving testimony because it might cost YOU too much. When God says, 'tonight's the night to share what I have redeemed', just do it. Because in these days ahead, you and I don't have the luxury of playing a "church lady" from late night television. This is not the time to get amnesia regarding the many instances where God has pulled us out of a pit, and by His grace, we've lived to tell about it. Instead, in these precious moments of time, OUR STORY could be a powerful catalyst to seeing another person set free! So be *willing* to go deeper if God asks it of you—knowing there is a Kingdom purpose in mind.

However, on the other hand, many of us have used the "power" of our stories to try and gain sympathy or garner attention for ourselves. What do I mean by that? Unfortunately, there have been times we have fallen prey to sharing our testimonies in such a way that God's redemptive power became a side note and our devastating circumstances the focal point. Without even realizing it, we over-share to either free ourselves of secret guilt that makes us feel unworthy in certain situations or we share with a hidden need for sympathy—both always falling flat and leaving others turned off. So before you tell your story to another, can I ask you a very important question? Who is the hero of your story? Is it you? Or is it God? Does it focus on what He did or is it laced with too many details of what "they" did? I have humbly learned—THROUGH EXPERIENCE— that it's usually best to tell just enough of our story to share our hearts and give credibility to our encouragement—but never so much that we're 'off in the weeds' to the point that the people listening are more caught up in OUR DRAMA than OUR SAVIOR.

Our testimonies are His stories to be used for His glory. So in this moment, give your 'sweet or tough', 'challenging yet victorious', or what may be a 'regretful but grace-filled' story BACK to a God who wants everyone in our path to experience His mercy. That's where the *power* of our story actually gets it power! In fact, ask The Lord to be the official narrator of the 'pages of GOLD' He's written on your behalf. It takes all of the pressure of saying 'too much' or 'too little' off of us when this becomes our heart's desire. Then instead of being full of false humility or racked with fear when an opportunity to share comes, we can experience the peace that passes all understanding—knowing and believing that the *details and timing* are God's and not ours.

My friend, you absolutely have a story worth telling. It's exciting to know that God is already orchestrating special opportunities for you to be a blessing to so many. My prayer is that every heartbreak in your life be redeemed for His glory. May each emerge as TREASURE to be shared with another who may be spiritually bankrupt and searching for the GOLD that now resides in you.

Heavenly Father, thank you for redeeming my life. Thank you that there is not one part of my story that cannot be used for your glory. Help me to remember that my past is my past. Shame and regret have no power over me once I allow you to control the narrative moving forward. I want to pray boldly today that You will send someone into my life who needs to hear my story. Give me courage to share the parts of my life that I have purposely kept buried because of pride or fear. Fill me with so much compassion that when I share the mercy You've shown me, it will look like GOLD to another desperate soul who needs to experience Your grace. Amen

STAY GOLD, FRIENDS!

Well, we have finished this chapter of our time together! We have allowed God to purify our hearts for weeks. We have asked Him to clean up our POTTY MOUTHS and GET OUR HANDS DIRTY. We have been challenged to RUN OUR RACE and at other times reminded to TAKE A SEAT. Sometimes we've had to LET IT GO while other times we've been told DON'T DROP THE BALL! The 24k Life is a rollercoaster! It's full of twists and turns—all personal encounters with Christ—designed to enrich our lives and the lives of those around us.

I hope you are beginning to see that God truly does not waste even one of the challenges we face each day. More importantly, I pray that you have developed a deeper understanding regarding the importance of *living out* your faith and that our time here on earth is not all about us. We are here to be light bearers that point others to an all powerful God. By applying God's perspective to our daily decisions, we tell them—through word and deed—about the redemptive love of Jesus Christ. When we choose to have a *day-to-day relationship* with Him, He composes a special narrative that becomes the framework of our calling here on earth.

So what do you say? Let's not stop here. Let's make a lifetime commitment to the refinement of our hearts. May they always be PURE GOLD in the hands of an Almighty God. Let's make reflecting His character our greatest goal and sharing His love our highest honor. May these words from the book of Job—that started our journey together—always keep us moving closer to the GOLD.

Here's to living the 24k Life!

"But He knows where I'm going. And when He tests me, I will come out as PURE GOLD...I have obeyed every word He's spoken, and not just obeyed His advice—I've treasured it."

JOB 23:10,11B NLT, THE MESSAGE

GETTING ETERNAL GOLD:
STEPS TO SALVATION

D o you desire to know the Lord's comforting presence? To experience His power? To understand His wisdom? That's awesome—because God loves you and wants to have a personal relationship with you too.

Why do you need a Savior?

There is only one thing that separates you from a relationship with Him—and that's sin. You and I sin—which means 'missing the mark'. Not one of us is able to hit a standard of perfection before a Holy God. We know that because Romans 3:23 tells us that we have all sinned and that we all fall short of the glory of God.

Romans 6:23 further explains that the penalty for sin is death—which is separation from God in hell FOREVER. The biggest problem we have is that no matter how hard we try, we cannot save ourselves or get rid of our sins. Ephesians 2:8-9 also reminds us that we can't earn our way to heaven by being good, going to church, or being baptized.

God wanted to bridge this gap because He loves us so much. His remedy for our sin—this sin that leaves us so helpless—was to send His only Son, Jesus, to save us.

Jesus Christ lived a perfect, sinless life, and then died on the cross to pay the penalty for our sins (Rom. 5:8). Three days later, He rose from the dead—showing that He had triumphed over sin and death once and for all.

Would you like to know God personally?

It all starts with accepting Jesus Christ as your Lord and Savior. Jesus Christ provides a relationship with the Father and eternal life through His death on the cross and resurrection (Rom. 5:10).

Romans 10:9 promises that "If you confess with your mouth that Jesus is Lord, and believe in your heart that God raised Him from the dead, you will be saved". If you have not yet begun your personal relationship with God, understand that the One who created you loves you no matter who you are or what you've done. He wants you to experience the profound depth of His care—right this minute.

This is a defining moment for you. Whisper to God, tell God that you are willing to trust Him for salvation. You can tell Him in your own words or use this simple prayer:

Lord Jesus, I ask You to forgive my sins and save me from eternal separation from God. By faith, I accept Your work and death on the cross as sufficient payment for my sins. Thank You for providing the way for me to know You and to have a personal relationship with my heavenly Father. Through faith in You, I believe that I now have eternal life. I believe that you have not only heard my prayers but also that you love me unconditionally. Please give me the strength, wisdom, and determination to seek your perspective in all I do and all I internalize from this day forward. In Jesus' name, AMEN.

If you prayed this prayer or a prayer of your own acknowledging Jesus Christ as your Savior, you just became a child of the King of Kings!!! Your new adventure as a believer in Christ begins today! You have made the best decision you will ever make—one that will change your life forever! Please let someone else know as soon as possible. Then make sure you get involved in a Bible-believing church!

You can also contact me at LeeAnnKirkindoll.com.
I would love to celebrate this decision with you!

LeeAnn Kirkindoll

L eeAnn Kirkindoll is a leader and communicator whose heart's desire is to enlighten women and girls of all ages on the importance of reflecting the light of Christ in their spheres of influence. She is the former Director of Women's Ministry at Prestonwood North Baptist Church as well as a nationally recognized children's room muralist featured in Better Homes and Gardens KIDS ROOM Magazine. Her love of art and design blossomed into a successful Proverbs 31 Business that eventually became her launching pad to encourage women.

As a leader and hands on teacher in ministry, she has been blessed to be a part of training, empowering and shepherding women entrusted to her for over 20 years. Her resume includes a passion for teaching bible studies, event planning, writing and leadership training. She is currently featured in the Embrace Grace DVD teaching curriculum and has enjoyed taking part in radio interviews, podcasts and women's conferences/ retreats throughout her professional tenure. Her eye for beautiful design has her knee deep in magazines, Pinterest pins, Instagram posts and ANY hard cover publications that feature women living out their passions by using their God-given gifts. However, her greatest earthly obsession is her family. LeeAnn and her husband Gary have 4 beautiful grown children, two amazing son-in-laws and 5 PRECIOUS GRANDSONS to date—soon to be 7!! They currently live in the relaxing Piney Woods of East Texas and are actively involved in their church home.

You can read and sign up to receive LeeAnn's blog, All Bright And Beautiful, at leeannkirkindoll.com. You can also stay encouraged by following her on FaceBook, Instagram and Pinterest.